LOST IN PLACE

RANDOM HOUSE NEW YORK

LOST IN PLACE

Growing Up Absurd in Suburbia

MARK SALZMAN

Grateful acknowledgment is made to Alfred A. Knopf, Inc., and Gower
Publishing Limited for permission to reprint excerpts from *Tao Te Ching* by
Lao Tsu, translated by Gia-fu Feng and Jane English. Copyright © 1972 by
Gia-fu Feng and Jane English. Rights throughout the British Commonwealth are
controlled by Gower Publishing Limited. Reprinted by permission of Alfred A.
Knopf, Inc. and Gower Publishing Limited.

Library of Congress Cataloging-in-Publication Data

Salzman, Mark.
Lost in place / Mark Salzman.—1st ed.
p.   cm.
ISBN 0-679-43945-5
1. Salzman, Mark—Childhood and youth.   2. Authors, American—20th
century—Biography.   3. Ridgefield (Conn. :Town)—Social life and customs.
I. Title.
PS3569.A4627Z473   1995
813'.54—dc20   95-7847

Manufactured in the United States of America
24689753
First Edition
Book design by JoAnne Metsch

For Joseph Arthur Salzman,
artist, astronomer, social worker, beloved father
and good-natured pessimist, whose reaction to this book
was to say that he enjoyed it, but felt that my portrayal
of him was inaccurate. I put him, he complained,
in an excessively positive light.

Although this is a work of nonfiction and represents the whole, unsullied, objective truth, I am advised of the slim chance that some of the people described in this book might remember things differently. To accommodate that absurd possibility, all of the names except for those of my immediate family have been changed.

The world is a hell of a place, but the universe is a fine thing.

          —EDWIN ARLINGTON ROBINSON

It has been asserted that we are destined to know the dark beyond the stars before we comprehend the nature of our own journey . . . but we also know that our inward destination lies somewhere a long way past the reef of the Sirens, who sang of knowledge but not of wisdom.

          —LOREN EISELY

LOST IN PLACE

1

When I was thirteen years old I saw my first kung fu movie, and before it ended I decided that the life of a wandering Zen monk was the life for me. I announced my willingness to leave East Ridge Junior High School immediately and give up all material things, but my parents did not share my enthusiasm. They made it clear that I was not to become a wandering Zen monk until I had finished high school. In the meantime I could practice kung fu and meditate down in the basement. So I immersed myself in the study of Chinese boxing and philosophy with the kind of dedication that is possible only when you don't yet have to make a living, when you are too young to drive and when you don't have a girlfriend.

First I turned our basement into what I thought a Buddhist temple should look like. I shoved all the junk to one side, marked off boundaries with candles and set up a shrine on a coffee table. I outfitted the shrine with objects from a cookware shop, the only store in town that carried Oriental gifts: a bamboo placemat, a package of chopsticks, a sake cup, which I turned into an incense burner, and a plastic Chinese kitchen deity with the character for "tasty" painted on his stomach. Next to the shrine I placed my sacred texts: the *World Book Encyclopedia* volumes containing entries for China, Buddhism and Taoism and Bruce Tegner's book *Kung Fu & Tai Chi*, seventh in a series of manuals by Mr. Tegner, a crew-cut ex-marine and our country's most prolific authority on hand-to-hand combat.

Back in those pre–smoke alarm days I was able to burn as much incense as I wanted, and as far as I was concerned a kung fu temple wasn't a kung fu temple if you could see more than five feet in front of you. Sadly, the only place in Ridgefield, Connecticut, where one could buy incense was a store called Ye Olde Head Shop, which specialized in black-light posters and rolling papers, and their incense display didn't feature traditional Asian scents like sandalwood or frankincense. Ye Olde Head Shop carried Apricot, Watermelon, Passion Fruit and something called Black Love, which came packaged in a long cardboard pouch illustrated with the silhouette of a naked man and woman, both with huge Afro haircuts, having sex. I did not dare ask the brooding hippie behind the counter for a pack of Black Love or even the more temperate-sounding Passion Fruit, so I stuck with the sexually neutral varieties, which did remind one of apricot and watermelon when you sniffed the box but as soon as you lit the cones smelled like burning cardboard.

There were other details. I needed an outfit for my training sessions, but the kung fu uniforms advertised in the martial arts magazines were too expensive. I settled on dyeing my green pajamas black, but the dye did not fix properly and my uniform came out an olive-purple. Tying it with my father's red bathrobe sash, I looked like an eggplant wrapped for Christmas. Trickiest of all, however, was what to do about my hair. Real Zen masters shave their heads, as anyone who has watched the *Kung Fu* series on television knows. My father had never liked my long hair, and had often said that he wished he could shave it all off, so I went directly to him and asked if he'd like to have a wish come true. His response was to raise one eyebrow, which I understood from experience to be a no.

As an alternative I ordered something called a Surprise Bald Head Wig from the back of a comic book. If, as advertised, it was good enough to surprise one's friends, I figured it would be good enough for my basement training sessions. When the wig arrived by mail four long weeks later, it turned out to be a disappointment. It was floppy, dimpled and a sickly gray color. I modified it by painting the reverse side of it with pink and orange Magic Markers, then powdering it with something out of my mother's cosmetics drawer. Eventually the wig did take on a fleshy appearance, but then I had to figure out what to do with all the hair my father had insisted on protecting, which stuck out from under the back and sides and hung down over my shoulders. My little brother, Erich, two years younger than I am, happened to wander into the bathroom before I had worked this problem out and declared that I looked more like Ebenezer Scrooge than "any of those bald guys on TV who wear dresses and kick people." My sister, Rachel, two years younger than Erich, thought I looked like a giant fetus. Not everyone felt about kung fu the way I did.

In the end I scrunched the extra hair up into a ball and stuffed it under the back of the wig. When I looked in the mirror I saw a determined young acolyte prepared to go through anything to achieve physical and spiritual mastery, but my parents, catching glimpses of me when I had to run upstairs to the bathroom, saw something else. The lumpy powdered head, the purple pajamas and the clouds of smoke that appeared behind me whenever I opened the basement door convinced them that I was headed for a career as a finger-cymbal player in airport lobbies.

That first summer of kung fu, while our family was in western Ohio visiting my mother's parents, Bruce Lee died. We were all having breakfast in the kitchen and my grandmother was calling my grandfather a "BB-brain" for having burned the toast yet again.

"Hold on," my father said, interrupting them and turning up the sound on their old black-and-white kitchen television set. It was on a tray with wheels so my grandmother could watch the news while she peeled potatoes, shucked corn, kneaded pie crust dough, washed the dishes or ironed clothes. "Look at this, Mark," my father said.

"The King of kung fu is dead at thirty-three!" the local newscaster announced. "Asia's biggest movie star died under mysterious circumstances in an actress's apartment in Hong Kong, on the eve of the release of his first American feature film. Here is a clip from one of his earlier movies." It was the famous scene from *The Chinese Connection* where Bruce jumps straight up into the air and kicks a wooden sign to pieces. That sign, a version of which actually did hang at the entrance to a park in foreign-occupied Shanghai earlier this century, had warned, NO DOGS OR CHINESE ALLOWED. That one scene made Bruce Lee a symbol of Chinese national pride over-night. It didn't matter that his character got executed by a firing squad at the end of the movie; the scene where he demolished the sign brought millions of ecstatic Chinese filmgoers to their feet and rocketed Bruce Lee to massive superstardom in Asia.

I couldn't believe he was dead. I went out to our car and sat in it all day, crying. My father felt so sorry for me he offered to take me all the way to Dayton to a drive-in movie theater that, by coincidence, was showing *The Chinese Connection*. We watched the movie together in the VW bus, my father trying to conceal his boredom while I burst into tears of joy and sorrow every time Bruce Lee started fighting. That night, after everyone else was asleep, I put on my wig and practiced in the dark living room, making silent but impassioned vows to my dead hero that I would never ever give up until I was an enlightened kung fu master myself.

Tutorials in Asian mysticism were not offered at East Ridge Junior High so I had to design my own course of study. From my research in the *World Book* I learned that the Buddha, while meditating under a tree just before dawn, happened to look up and see Venus rising in the eastern sky. Somehow this vision of the shining planet helped him to achieve nirvana, a state of mind described as the emancipation from all suffering. I interpreted this literally and became convinced that Buddhism was all about becoming oblivious to pain. Building up an immunity to discomfort became my spiritual goal, and toward this end I made my Zen and kung fu practice as uncomfortable as I could. On sunny days I meditated in the crawl space; on rainy days I sat outdoors in the mud. I made sure that all of my stretching, punching and kicking exercises hurt, which any good athlete could have told me was a bad idea, but I hadn't asked any athletes for their advice. Meditation for me involved trying to concentrate on "emptiness"—a squirmingly unpleasant challenge for any thirteen-year-old—while my crossed legs ached and my nose itched.

I didn't realize it at the time, but there was a fundamental difference between what I was doing and what most real Buddhists do. The Buddha himself abandoned a comfortable life because he could not stand the hypocrisy of being a chubby prince when there was so much suffering all around him. He made himself homeless and destitute first and then sought nirvana because he figured that it was worth seeking only if it was available to even the poorest person on earth. I, on the other hand, wanted to become a Zen master because I hoped perfect enlightenment would make me more popular—specifically, more datable. As the youngest and shortest boy in my class, I was convinced that I would go to my grave without having sex unless I did something extraordinary with my life. Although it may be true these days that you can't throw a rock in America without hitting a psychic or a Tibetan lama or a yoga instructor, in 1973 becoming a Zen student in Ridgefield qualified as extraordinary. I hoped that if I became a living Buddha, I would never again have to hear the words "You're just like a little brother to me" when I asked someone on a date.

Then there was kung fu. From the movies and television programs I saw, I gathered that one of the key benefits of being a Buddhist monk was that you could beat the crap out of bad people without getting emotionally involved or physically tired. You were always on the moral high ground because you were a pacifist, but if someone was foolish enough to throw a punch at you anyway, surprise! Kung fu turned you into a cross between Sugar Ray Robinson, Mikhail Baryshnikov and Mahatma Gandhi. My hope was to impose this surprise on at least one of the eighth-grade assholes who used to pick on me for being tiny, polite to adults and a cellist in a youth orchestra.

Last but not least, I wanted to become a Zen master because I thought it would impress my father. Like most boys, I wanted to prove myself by doing something my father couldn't do, but also like most boys, I thought my dad could do anything. He could drive, paint, name the constellations, set up a tent and had been in the air force—what else was there? The answer came the first night I saw David Carradine, about to be ambushed by a gang of murderous cowboys, sit cross-legged on the ground and play his bamboo flute. I could hardly contain my excitement; this was definitely something my dad couldn't do.

If my dad knew he was about to be ambushed by murderous cowboys, first he would shake his head with disgust and say that he knew all along that something like this would happen to him. Then he would pace back and forth for a while, muttering curse words and wondering aloud at the foolishness of people who romanticize the Wild West. Finally he would resign himself to the inevitable, consoling himself with the thought that his murderers, like everyone else in the world, would die soon enough, the sun would eventually grow cold and all of this madness would be mercifully consigned to oblivion. It was not difficult for me to imagine this scenario; my dad played out a version of it whenever a faucet leaked, the furnace made a strange sound or an odd smell came out of the engine compartment of our car. You could almost see the first ugly thought when it appeared—"We're going to have to buy a whole new sink/heating system/car now"—as if it were scrawled onto the muscles of his jaw, and then you watched it spread until his whole body was covered with despairing graffiti. My father experienced serene detachment only when he was asleep and not having nightmares about the plumbing, the car or being in college again.

I knew that if I became an unflappable sage my father would be both proud and envious of me, and he would have to admit that the baldhead wig and pajamas had been good ideas after all. So while most of my junior high classmates began asserting themselves through academics, sports or troublemaking, I decided to follow in the footsteps of the ancient masters, whose knowledge was described in the fifth century B.C. classic *Tao Te Ching* as:

> . . . *unfathomable.*
> *Because it is unfathomable,*
> *All we can do is describe their appearance.*
> *Watchful, like men crossing a winter stream.*
> *Alert, like men aware of danger.*
> *Courteous, like visiting guests.*
> *Yielding, like ice about to melt.*
> *Simple, like uncarved blocks of wood.*
> *Hollow, like caves.*
> *Opaque, like muddy pools.*

When I read this passage aloud to my father to acquaint him with my new philosophy, he didn't respond immediately. He pushed his coffee cup across the kitchen table, first to the left, then to the right, then tried to center it in front of him. When he did this it usually meant he was about to deliver a sobering lecture. I steeled myself for his gentle but devastatingly rational critique of the unfathomable knowledge of old, but it never came. He found a satisfactory place for the cup, nodded in a way that I knew meant he wasn't enthusiastic but wasn't going to rain on my parade either, then said, "My son, the block of wood. Let me know if it works."

My dad always saw things a bit too clearly for his own good. His gift for imagining all that could go wrong in any situation earned him the nickname Little Old Joe by the time he was five. One of his older brothers told me that my father did not seem to experience childhood so much as to bear it; his face seemed to have been frozen at birth into an expression of weary stoicism. He enhanced this reputation for seeming older than his years by spending evenings gazing out his bedroom window at the night sky, memorizing the constellations and watching for northern lights displays. He exhausted the library's collection of books about the stars and planets, and subscribed to *Sky and Telescope* magazine before entering high school. This interest in astronomy mystified his parents, who were both decidedly earthbound characters. My grandmother once described herself to me as a nice girl from Texas whose job was to raise four boys, and my grandfather was a no-nonsense contractor who paved the first McDonald's restaurant parking lot.

Unlike many prodigies whose gifts fade at an early age, my father never lost his talent for seeing things in a stark light. Fortunately he discovered painting, through which he managed to express himself with great success. Unfortunately, that same gift made him too disparaging of his bleak paintings to promote them, so rather than starve in a loft he became a social worker. He reasoned that if he couldn't do what he enjoyed for a living, he could at least do something beyond reproach, and in any case psychology had been the subject in college that interested him most. Not surprisingly, given his personality, he turned out to be a sympathetic listener and was highly regarded throughout his career, but if you asked him about his work, he would tell you only that social services were fighting a losing battle. He was often depressed himself in spite of all he knew about psychology and the mind, although he would say it was *because* of all he knew about psychology and the mind. Every morning he left the house looking as if someone had tied a hundred-pound sandbag across his shoulders, and every evening he came back looking as if the sand had gotten wet. He never mentioned his work unless he was asked about it, and we kids knew better than to ask.

In fact, for some time I was confused about what he did during the day; the misunderstanding came about one winter morning when, after having gotten up before dawn to put an electric heating blanket over the engine of our Volkswagen (otherwise it wouldn't start in the winter) before his hour-long commute, he came into the house to savor a final moment of warmth and said to no one in particular, "Back to the salt mines." I overheard this and went on to announce during show-and-tell that my daddy worked underground; on the back of my report card that year my teacher, who knew that my father was not a miner, wrote, "I worry that sometimes Mark seems to be in his own little world."

She was right. I *was* in my own little world, and it consisted mostly of daydreaming to pass the time until Daddy came home from work. For me that was when real life began, because I adored my gloomy father. He was fairly strict, did not care for board games, owned no power tools and had no interest in sports, but he was great company. Aristotle observed that melancholy men are the most witty, to which I would add that they are also the most fun to confide in. For much of my young life I enjoyed nothing better than to help him forget about his awful day at work by telling him about my awful day at school, and this usually led to a good meandering conversation. Sometimes we talked sitting on the living-room floor because that was where he painted, with half of his materials in boxes scattered all around him and the other half ground into the rug. On weekends we talked in the car on the way to the town dump, to the hardware store, to the Volkswagen dealer or to my Youth Symphony rehearsals in Norwalk. If the weather was too awful, he would declare it a Green Blanket Day, pull out an ancient, tattered green blanket, throw it on one of our collapsed sofas, make cinnamon toast and tea for Erich, Rachel and me and spend the day napping there with us and telling stories. Occasionally I joined him for his morning walk around the dairy farm near our house because I could count on his wanting to chat rather than keep his mind on exercise, which he hated. Most of all, though—and most enjoyable of all—we talked under the stars during our astronomy sessions.

Sensing I might be an eager disciple, my dad started me on the hobby as soon as I was old enough to stay awake past eight o'clock. My earliest childhood memory is of his taking me out to a cold field in the middle of the night to see comet Ikeya-Seki. This was in 1965. From its bright starlike head to the end of its frosty tail it measured over thirty million miles, which represents one third of the distance from the earth to the sun. The comet glowed so brightly in the cold night air that the cows standing near us looked like ghostly worshipers, forming icons of their deity with their own breath. As we stamped our feet to keep warm, my father told me that comets were really not much more than snowballs, and that each time they passed by the sun they melted a little. "In a few hundred million years," he said, "that comet we're looking at will melt completely, and the dust from the tail will be blown by the solar wind out into the space between the stars."

One reason, I think, that conversations while stargazing can be so memorable is that you can't really see your companion's face. You can only hear his voice while staring up into the darkness, which brings the words into unusually sharp focus. When I asked my dad what would happen to the dust from the tail after it got blown out of the solar system, he said, "Well, gravity might catch it and pull it into a huge cloud of other kinds of dust, and then it would become a new star or planet. Or it might drift out in space forever."

"How can it drift forever?"

He paused before answering, "Nobody knows, really. But you'll have a better idea once you get a job."

Ironically, the one job my dad talked about with enthusiasm required drifting in space; he knew the names of all the astronauts, and considered every one of them a hero. Not surprisingly, when I was seven years old (around the middle of the Gemini program) I decided that I had to become an astronaut. I didn't mean when I grew up, however; I meant right then, preferably by the end of the month. When I told my father this he said, "You're too young to be an astronaut right this minute, but if you keep working hard at your schoolwork, you could have a chance at it someday." This advice discouraged me, but my mother saved the day by suggesting that I write a letter to NASA asking for information about the astronaut program; who knows, she said, maybe there was something I could do right away, even as a seven-year-old.

"Oh, Martha," my father said, shaking his head. "They don't have time to answer mail like that."

"It doesn't hurt to try," she countered angrily, so I did write a letter, and three weeks later received a large manila envelope from NASA stuffed with color photographs from space and pamphlets about the space program. "You see?" asked Mom, who never seemed surprised when her long-shot suggestions worked. "You should never be afraid to try something!"

Taking her advice, I began my astronaut training immediately. One of the pamphlets showed an astronaut tucked inside a cramped mock capsule, and the text below explained that the astronauts had to get used to spending many long hours without being able to move. In an early display of what was to become my trademark habit—the obsessive pursuit of unrealistic goals—I decided to set a record for sitting still in a cramped space. I was sure this would get NASA's attention.

I found a cardboard box that I could barely fit into, drew buttons and gauges all over the inside of it and outfitted it with a blanket, a thermometer, an alarm clock and a periscope made with two of my mother's compact mirrors. I set up the space photo from NASA against the wall so I could look at them through the periscope and imagine myself on a real mission. My ground crew—Erich and Rachel—prepared Dixie cups filled with sugar water for me and passed them down through the periscope hole when I needed more energy. I began the program by sitting in the box for half an hour, and increased my time every day by adding ten minutes. When I got to over an hour a day it started to get boring, but I knew I had to push on. If I was chosen for the real thing, a trip to the moon, think how long I would have to be prepared to sit!

I knew it was important that I not be comfortable, so I did not allow myself a cushion to sit on, and kept the box closed at all times so that it would get stuffy and overheated. Once a training session began I did not let myself out to go to the bathroom. After a week or so, when I felt my determination waning, I started pointing the box toward the TV so I could watch my favorite program—*Lost in Space*—through the periscope to counteract the boredom.

I did this for several weeks, building up to over three hours per session before the training came to an abrupt end. I remember the last mission well:

"Mission Commander—this is Mission Control in Houston. Prepare for Trans-Lunar Injection."

"Mission Commander here. All systems go. Preparing for the burn."

"Ten seconds until ignition."

The Trans-Lunar Injection would take me out of the earth's orbit and send me toward the moon. It would increase my speed from seventeen thousand miles an hour to more than twenty-five thousand miles an hour.

"Ignition!"

There was no sensation of acceleration, no noise and just a slight vibration. Only my computer told me that I was picking up speed at a phenomenal rate. When the burn finished, the vibration stopped.

"Burn complete."

After that, all was silent. I was in deep space now. The capsule was stuffy and hot inside; a look at the thermometer told me it was 95 degrees. The alarm clock indicated I had been inside it for three hours and five minutes. Suddenly I heard a pop, and felt myself shift in position. Another pop, but this was a little longer in duration, and sounded more like something tearing. Oh no! One of the welded seams of the capsule was opening! If it got any wider, I would lose all air pressure! My body would pop like an overinflated balloon, then freeze instantly in the absolute vacuum of space.

"Mayday, Mayday!" I shouted. "Mission Control, this is Mission Commander. We have a problem."

"Honey, I'm teaching now."

What?

"Where did that voice come from, Mrs. Salzman?"

"Oh, from that box over there near the TV. My son's in it."

Mayday! Mayday! I turned the periscope around and saw, instead of the earth or moon or the limitless void, a sight that confused me. It was my mother, giving a piano lesson in our living room, and her student was sitting on the bench, staring in my direction.

"He's practicing to be an astronaut," my mother explained in a stage whisper. "He puts those pictures of the stars in front of the box and looks at them through the little periscope. He's been doing it for weeks now." She looked toward me. "Oops! Honey, I think your box is starting to fall apart. Your rear end is sticking out." Her student giggled.

My butt had popped out of the spaceship, right in front

of one of Mom's teenage piano students. I was seven years old again.

I pulled the toy periscope down, climbed out through the top and carefully avoided looking at either my mother or her student. My face was tingling, which I knew meant that it was red as a baboon's ass. I went upstairs to my room, lay down on the bed and prepared for the arrival of what I called the Black Fog, which descended whenever I came out of an outstanding daydream and realized that I was still a little kid in Connecticut. This time the Black Fog hung over me for weeks. It lifted only when my father brought home a book called *Mammals Do the Strangest Things,* which inspired my next unrealistic project: turning the swamp in our front yard into a platypus, fruit bat and armadillo sanctuary.

In spite of my failure to become an astronaut, I continued to enjoy astronomy lessons with my father, and our stargazing chats ensured my never losing touch with his dark sense of humor. By the time I reached my teens I had learned the secret of his way of thinking, which was to acknowledge, as Tolstoy had, that the only thing we can really know is that we know nothing. Tolstoy considered this to be the highest flight of human reason, whereas for my dad it was just another grim fact and the only possible explanation for the success of phenomena like the Spanish Inquisition, paintings on black velvet of sad clowns and country-western music. He regarded Woody Allen as a sociologist first and a comedian second; he felt that Edvard Munch would have made a better psychiatrist than Sigmund Freud; and he agreed with Arthur Koestler, who wrote that the human brain was perhaps the only example of evolution providing a species with an organ it does not know how to use.

My only complaint about my father's pessimism was that he didn't get more pleasure out of it. This revealed the biggest difference between him and me, the one gap that not even a lifetime of conversation could bridge: my father was a natural pessimist who expected the worst as a matter of course, while I am a synthetic pessimist, someone who tries to protect himself from disappointment by convincing himself that pessimists have the right idea. Natural pessimists suffer when their harsh predictions come true, whereas synthetic pessimists get a kick out of being right for a change. I felt more alive talking with my dad about death than I did listening to other people speculate about immortality, and the satisfaction I felt when he helped me find the right words to articulate a problem buoyed me up higher than any pep talk could have. From my own experiences as a manufactured curmudgeon, then, it seemed to me that my father should have been the liveliest, most buoyant man in the world. The reality was that he was unhappy much of the time, and this left me confused.

I was unhappy a lot of the time, but I could think of good reasons for this. I was a kid and, like all kids, was not really living my own life. School, homework, meals, cello lessons, manners, transportation and hygiene were all factors determined by the law, the establishment or my parents and it was useless to resist. Plus I was physically small, which virtually guarantees misery in boys. I clung to the idea that if I made it to twenty-one alive and without a long criminal record I would be rewarded with independence, a growth spurt, a steady companion of the opposite sex, my own car and a paying job. Then I could be a happy pessimist all day long, not just in the evenings and on weekends when Daddy was home.

My father threatened this vision of paradise. He was married, tall, salaried, drove his own Volkswagen bus and knew there was no point in getting too worked up over what one read about in the papers, yet he was depressed, particularly from Monday morning to Friday afternoon. I felt bad for him, but somewhere around the beginning of adolescence I realized his angst created an opening for me, an opportunity to carve out an identity of my own without hurting or disappointing him: all I had to do was become happy. If I accomplished this he would have to be impressed and might even ask me how I did it, putting me in the position of giving him advice for a change.

Somewhere in that pilot episode of the *Kung Fu* series I watched, the character who became everyone's favorite— Master Po, the blind monk who could hear grasshoppers walk—described enlightenment as a sense of oneness with the universe. That was the moment I knew I had to find out more about it; that was when I became convinced that whoever invented kung fu must have had me in mind. Given my background as an astronomer's apprentice, it was hard for me to imagine a nobler or more intriguing way of becoming happy than by merging with the night sky. If it worked for Buddha, who became enlightened when his eyes fell on Venus, it might work for me. And I couldn't help noticing that Buddhism offered a blend of pessimism and idealism wonderfully suited to my circumstances: Buddha recognized all life as suffering and ignorance and gave up his stake in the world as we know it, but by doing so, he came to live in a state of perpetual euphoria. So when my dad told me to let him know if becoming like a block of wood worked, there was no turning back. I had to become at one with the universe because to return from such a queer but promising journey empty-handed would have been too humiliating.

2

After several months passed and I had made no apparent progress toward becoming hollow like a cave or opaque like a muddy pool, I decided to pick up the pace. I endeavored to use every moment of the day as a kind of training, not just the hours when I was meditating or practicing kung fu. Still thinking that becoming impervious to pain was the key to enlightenment, I started pinching myself a lot during class, skipping meals, wearing too much or too little clothing for the weather and walking barefoot to school. This last training method sorely tested Erich and Rachel's loyalty because every time they passed me while riding the bus to school they had to hear the other kids laughing about the idiot with no shoes on.

Being the oldest child, I often wondered what it would have been like to have an older brother. When I pictured him, I usually saw in my mind a cool guy with long hair who sneaked me into bars with his friends, introduced me to girls and taught me to play electric bass so that I could join his rock band. Only now, when I think of what my real-life siblings had to go through, do I realize how lucky I was that I could make my imaginary older brother disappear at will. Besides having to see me wander around the house in a baldhead wig and pajamas or sitting cross-legged out in the backyard in the rain, they had to put up with my requests that they hold duffel bags full of clothes for me to punch and kick, shoot arrows at me with Dad's bow so that I could practice dodging skills or tug on ropes tied around my ankles to get my legs to stretch further. For Erich, however, the bare feet in winter was just too much—he broke the code of silence and tattled on me. My parents gave me a spirited lecture that night, and the next morning my mother made sure I left the house with shoes on. In addition, she made me promise to keep them on until I came home. I kept my promise, but outsmarted her by cutting the soles out of the shoes, which prompted my ever-observant French teacher to take me aside one day and ask, "Mark, haven't you ever heard of Shoetown?"

Eager for more advanced training methods, I read an article in a martial arts magazine claiming that back in the old days kung fu masters had trained themselves not to urinate. The magazine explained that those great masters stood crouched in the horse stance (the fundamental posture for most Asian martial arts) for eight or ten hours at a time, sweating out toxins and using their amazing psychic powers to transform what was left in their bladders into powerful *ch'i,* translated in the article as "internal life-force breath essence." I gave retention a try, but only for one afternoon; some of the secrets of old, I concluded, had been lost forever.

A year after seeing that first kung fu program I entered

high school, and I was restless. I could imitate all of the movements described in *Bruce Tegner's Book of Kung Fu and Tai Chi,* but felt no closer to being a martial arts master. Every day I meditated with my legs crossed for as long as it took a cone of apricot incense to burn down to the coffee table, but instead of concentrating on emptiness I spent most of that time trying not to imagine what my female classmates looked like naked. Most annoying of all, early symptoms of chronic back strain—brought on by my technique of suddenly jumping up into the air and kicking without stretching or warming up to practice being "alert, like men aware of danger"—reminded me all day long that I had not conquered pain. I needed a real teacher. Discouraged and frustrated, I asked my parents why I had to wait five years before I could join a Zen monastery, and they repeated that it was important to have a high school degree. But, they said, if I could find a kung fu school they would drive me to lessons.

"There aren't any kung fu schools in Connecticut," I moaned.

"Are you sure? Have you checked the Yellow Pages?" my mother asked. This was typical advice from my mother, a classical musician who approached all tasks with the same cheerful thoroughness. To her every day teemed with welcome challenges; she couldn't see how anyone could feel bored. The days never seemed long enough to her, and she couldn't understand why a person would lounge around in bed in the morning when instead they could pop out from under those covers and start accomplishing things. In short, she was the exact opposite of my father. She rarely indulged in philosophical speculation, but never tired of stating the two basic principles according to which she lived and worked: If you are busy you won't have time to complain, and if you ever have a question, you should immediately look it up in the *World Book*, the *Harvard Music Dictionary* or the Yellow Pages.

As usual I scoffed at her suggestion—she might as well have told me to look for incense at Sears—but just to make sure, when she wasn't looking I took the phone book downstairs into the basement and checked under kung fu. *See Martial Arts Instruction*, the book advised. I opened to the *M* section, and to my astonishment, just beneath *Marital Aids*, I found a listing that contained this ad: *Chinese Boxing Institute, House of Kung Fu.*

My mother drove me there the next evening. On the way, trying to sound casual, she said, "You know, if this doesn't turn out to be the teacher you want, don't get discouraged. Sometimes it takes time to find the right person."

"What makes you say that, Mom?"

"Well . . . it's just that the man who runs this place didn't sound very friendly over the phone."

My heart stopped. "What do you mean, he didn't sound very friendly. You talked to him?"

"Well, it's only right to make an appointment before you go to a teacher, Mark. At least that's how it's done with music lessons—the mothers of my new students always call first and make an appointment for a first lesson. That way I know what level the student is at and I can be prepared."

"What did you say to him?" I asked. I had a bad feeling about this telephone call.

"Well, I told him you'd been practicing very hard on your own for a year, so you wouldn't be starting as a beginner, and he sort of shouted at me."

"Oh, my God—"

"Don't worry, Mark, he was just mad at me, not at you."

"What did he say?"

"Well, he said, 'Everybody starts as a beginner in my school!' Actually, he kind of shouted it. Which is fine. But, Mark, if his karate isn't what you had in mind—"

"It's *kung fu,* Mom!"

"Of course—kung fu. If it's not what you want, just remember that there are always other teachers out there. You might have to keep looking."

I rode the rest of the way in silence. Adolescence is not a reasonable time; in my mind she might as well have told the kung fu master I wouldn't be needing diapers since I was already fourteen.

At last we arrived at the Chinese Boxing Institute, a small brick building adjacent to a cemetery. Through the large picture window I could see six or seven tough-looking men with beards and mustaches, all wearing black outfits and stretching out on the floor under a wall display of swords and throwing knives. I begged my mother not to come in with me. She seemed to understand and said, "All right, I'll come back in two hours. Have fun!" She dropped me off and turned around for the forty-five-minute drive home.

I opened the door and shuffled in, clutching my purple pajamas tightly against my chest. Looking around, I noticed that the paneling on the wall was crushed in several places, obviously from bodies being hurled against it, and the whole place reeked of sweat and bare feet. A tiny Oriental-style wooden bridge separated the entrance from the workout area. On the far side of the room were three doors, one marked MEN, one marked WOMEN, and the third marked OFFICE. I could hear a small commotion taking place in the office; large objects were being shuffled and bumped around and occasionally a woman giggled.

A huge man, six feet tall and indestructible-looking, walked over to greet me. He had short, curly brown hair, a handlebar mustache, a boxer's nose and a gaze so intense it made my knees shake. The sleeves of his uniform were rolled way up, revealing a dark tattoo on his arm of a bearded man with a beret smoking a joint. His biceps, I noticed, were the size of my thighs, and his hands appeared to have been chiseled out of granite blocks. He was the scariest-looking man I had ever seen.

"Are you Master O'Keefe?" I asked.

"Nope. I'm Bill. The Master's in there," he said, gesturing toward the office. "What can I do for you?" I noticed that his face showed no expression at all; he seemed neither interested in me nor annoyed, so I pressed on.

"I—I'm here for the kung fu class. Should I come some other time?"

"Nope. You bring a uniform?"

"Yes—sort of. It's not a real uniform."

"That should be fine. Why don't you go put it on?"

I crossed the bridge—"You gotta bow when you cross the bridge," Bill advised me—then went into the dressing room. There were two more grown men in there wearing nothing but jockstraps. I froze with embarrassment; it was the first time I had ever been in a dressing room, and had not taken my pants off in front of anyone since being a toddler. I felt myself blush, but the two men didn't comment on it. As I unbuttoned my shirt, one of them asked, "Hey, how old are you, kid?"

"Fourteen."

"Jesus, don't you think you oughta be in the kids' class? Sensei teaches one in the afternoon, you know."

I shrugged. I did not want to be in the kids' class. I put on my pajama bottoms as fast as I could, but one of the men said, "Hey, aren't you gonna wear a strap?"

"Oh . . . I don't have one."

They both laughed. "What are you gonna do when you get kicked in the balls? You get kicked in the balls all the time doin' this, kid. You better get yourself a jock soon, or your voice isn't ever gonna change."

They left the dressing room before I had finished changing. By the time I had tied the red bathroom sash around my eggplant costume, I was ready to go home, but there was no turning back—I had to go out there.

When I pulled the sliding door to one side and came out into the brightly lit room, all eyes turned to greet me.

"Jesus Christ, look at this! A red sash! He's a master already! And a purple *gi!* Get the camera!"

Thankful that I had chosen not to bring the bald wig, I noticed that Bill, the scary-looking one who had greeted me at the door, was not laughing. He signaled me to approach him, fixing me with his unnervingly steady gaze. I thought he was going to tell me to change back into my street clothes and come back on kiddie afternoon, but instead he said in a low voice, "They're laughin' now, but if you stick with it, you might be kicking their asses in a couple years, and who'll be laughin' then?" He seemed to grin, but it was hard to be sure. Only an effort of will prevented me from bursting into tears of gratitude. Before I could thank him, however, he grew serious and said, "You'd better take that red sash off, though. Sensei wouldn't like that much, and you don't want to get him pissed, believe me." I ripped it off and would have eaten it if Bill had told me to. Then he advised me to go over to the office, tell the Master that I had arrived and ask permission to join the class.

"But it sounds like he's, um, busy," I protested.

"Aw, he ain't busy," Bill said, appearing to grin again. "Just knock first."

I walked across the room and stood in front of the sliding door. I could still hear a woman giggling inside. The men who had laughed at me earlier were now urging me with silent gestures to go ahead, knock on the door! They all seemed to expect something funny to happen. When I knocked, an angry voice yelled out, *"What the fuck?"*

"I . . . I . . ."

Before I could answer, the door slid open and a young woman, also dressed in a black kung fu uniform, trotted out. She flashed me a pleasant but quizzical look as she passed. I tiptoed into the office, trying to make myself look as small as possible, and gazed at the Master for the first time. He was sitting with his feet propped up on a desk, under rows and rows of shelves covered with enormous, shiny karate trophies. The walls were covered with certificates and photographs of himself breaking stacks of flaming bricks, grimacing, flourishing weapons and flying through the air.

Sensei O'Keefe was much smaller and thinner than I had expected—he couldn't have weighed more than one hundred and twenty pounds, and was not much taller than I was—had deep-set eyes with heavy shadows under them behind aviator-style glasses, a handlebar mustache with a Fu Manchu beard growing down from under his lower lip, and teeth that had clearly been rearranged several times during the course of his journey to mastery. He wore three-inch-high wooden-heeled disco boots, bell-bottom hip-hugger pants, a tight-fitting half-shirt that revealed his belly button and was attached to his pants with gaudy chain-link suspenders, a gold chain around his neck and a wide-brimmed leather hat with coins set around the rim. He had rings on several of his fingers, but most prominent was one shaped like a dragon curled around an oval jade stone. He looked like a white character from a black exploitation movie from the seventies—not at all what I had expected. He also looked angry.

"Are you the one," he boomed, "whose mother called and said you were too good to start as a beginner?"

I couldn't even speak.

"Well, let's get something straight, Mr. Salzman. I am the Master of this house, and in this house, I say who starts where, not anybody else, and not anybody's mommy. Is that clear?"

"Yes, sir."

He glared at me so severely and with such intense loathing that I became dizzy. "All right, then," he said, looking away as if he could stand the sight of me no longer. "Here are the registration forms. How old are you?"

"Fourteen."

I was sure he was going to tell me either to go home or to come back for the kiddie class.

"In that case, take 'em home to your parents to sign." He handed me a few sheets of paper that explained when the class met, what it would cost, and how I was not to hold the Master responsible if I got hurt. "And get a uniform like everybody else. If I want you in designer colors, I'll let you know."

"Yes, sir. Thank you, sir."

I fled out of the office, bowed on my way over the bridge and went straight to the parking lot. I intended to wait there for the two hours in my pajamas until my mother came to pick me up, but then the door opened and Bill stuck his head out. "Hey, Grasshopper, Sensei says you can follow along tonight. Come on."

I joined him, the other men and the giggly young woman in loose formation in the center of the workout room. The Master stalked out of his office and went into the dressing room, his suspenders making a delicate tinkling sound. A few minutes later he exploded through the door, wearing a black uniform with a faded black belt that had five white bands on it—a fifth-degree black belt! Embroidered on the back of the uniform were the letters *AKMF*. I assumed they stood for American Kung Fu Masters' Federation, but Bill later explained that they stood for Ass-Kicking Motherfucker.

"Line up!" the Master screamed, and all took their places in three parallel lines. Bill pointed to the farthest corner spot in the rear line, and I hustled there. The Master did not look pleased with us, however.

"When I say line up," he seethed, "I don't mean I want a bunch of goddamned pussies strolling around and bumping into each other! *I mean I want to see you move!* Hit the ground, goddammit!" Everybody fell face forward and started doing push-ups on their knuckles, and I followed suit. We kept at it until the Master yelled again, "Line up!" and we all moved as if we had just heard a gunshot. Satisfied this time, the Master had us all bow to him, then led everyone through a little prayer:

> *"Kung fu is my secret,*
> *I bear no arms.*
> *May the Lord forgive me,*
> *If I should use my hands."*

Then he looked right at me, frowning. Though the other students were facing away from me, I noticed that they all were looking at me via the reflection in the mirrors on the far wall. All of a sudden I realized how physically small I was compared with the other students. I was not yet five feet tall and weighed barely one hundred pounds, and for a moment the kiddie class seemed like not such a bad idea after all.

The Master's face broke into a grin. "Since Mr. Salzman brought his pajamas," he said, "we ought to give him a chance. Does anybody object to his joining the class?"

"No!" all those grown men yelled enthusiastically. They turned to look at me and their expressions were genuinely friendly. Apparently, by not complaining or starting to cry I had passed their test and was now OK.

"All right, then," the Master said, nodding at me. "If you get lost, just keep up the count with front punches and don't worry about it. Let's get this fucking show on the road. Basic techniques, count out twenty, starting at this corner."

My heart nearly burst with joy. I forgot about the Master's suspenders, the hip huggers and the giggling girl, and vowed to go through any physical or mental pain, any injury or indignity, to prove myself in his eyes. I realized with devastating clarity that I had always been a sissy— playing the cello! astronomy! baldhead wigs in the basement! But now that I'd found a man who feared nothing, whom I had just seen reduce a group of burly men to trembling obedience with a single command—*who had to ask God to forgive him for what he could do with his bare hands!*—now things were going to change.

3

___

Given that I was now spending most of my free time pursuing a state of mind that was "empty, containing nothing, and therefore full, containing everything," this became the subject of most of my conversations with my father. I can only imagine how much he must have wished I had gotten interested in painting instead. My biggest complaint at this time was having to spend so many hours at school memorizing facts that were of no interest to me. It wasn't just that I would have been happier spending that time practicing kung fu; I believed that the knowledge I was gaining in school was actively preventing me from becoming a master.

"What makes you think that, Mark?" Dad asked. That night we were setting up the telescope on the same field we had stood in to watch comet Ikeya-Seki nearly ten years earlier. Our goal this time was to find the Horsehead Nebula, a glowing cloud of hydrogen in the constellation Orion.

All true scientists possess a childlike sense of wonder, but I think that astronomers have to be the most childlike of all. Everything they study dwarfs them, in terms both of size and of longevity, and most of what they observe is hopelessly out of reach. No human being can visualize the distance that light travels in one year, much less the distance it travels in two million years, which is how far you would have to travel to reach the major galaxy *nearest* to our own.

Children lie on their backs and see familiar objects in the shapes of clouds; astronomers look through gigantic lenses and see familiar objects in the shapes of galaxies, the vast, rarefied clouds of hydrogen that form the nurseries for new stars, and the expanding bubbles of heavy atoms and radiation left behind when stars die in cataclysmic explosions. A map of the night sky reads like a kid's wish list of good things to hide in a drawer: the Crab Nebula, the Sombrero Galaxy, the Dumbbell Nebula, the Beehive Cluster, the Owl Nebula and a galaxy known simply as the Tarantula.

To answer my father's question about why I thought high school was ruining my mind, I told him that Lao-tse, the fifth century B.C. Taoist philosopher and author of the *Tao Te Ching*, had advised people to "stop learning and end your problems."

Dad looked unimpressed. "That's it? Stop learning and end your problems? That's a whole philosophy?"

"That's only part of it, Dad. Duh!"

"Don't say 'duh,' Mark, it's so annoying."

"Well, you're trying to make this stuff sound stupid!

It's only been around for two thousand years, and I think there's probably something to it."

"OK, OK. So why would stopping learning end your problems?"

I fetched my copy of the *Tao Te Ching* out of the car and read in the purplish light just before nightfall,

"In the pursuit of learning, every day something is acquired.
In the pursuit of Truth, every day something is dropped.

Less and less is done
Until non-action is achieved.
When nothing is done, nothing is left undone.

The world is ruled by letting things take their course.
It cannot be ruled by interfering."

My father had a special kind of laugh that he reserved for matters that struck him as funny in one way but unfunny in another. It was not a snort so much as a fast sigh.

"Mark, how is a person supposed to live according to that philosophy? Who's going to pay your food and heating bills if you don't do anything?"

I knew there had to be a good answer to his question, but the problem was that you had to be enlightened to know the real answer, and I wasn't enlightened. I was fourteen years old and had not yet learned that "I don't know" is a viable answer to profound questions. I took evasive action and told him that the reason he couldn't understand was precisely that he had gone through all that social conditioning and so-called education that he, my mother and the Connecticut public school system were now forcing upon me.

He gave me the special laugh again and said, "Yeah, yeah, but let me hear *you* explain what *you think* it means. Even if I can't understand it, I'll be interested in hearing this."

Seeing that I had no choice but to try to guess what an enlightened person would say, I responded, "You didn't listen, Dad! It says that *when nothing is done, nothing is left undone,* so everything actually does get done. It's just that it's, like, effortless. You don't have to struggle because everything you do happens naturally. It's like the way a cat does stuff. A cat doesn't wake up and say, 'Oh, damn, I've gotta go to work today.' It just, like, *is,* without worrying about it."

Dad finished bolting the telescope tube to the stand and looked around his feet. "I think the eyepiece box is still in the car," he said. "You want to go get it?"

It was a familiar strategy of his to find a casual diversion to give him time to think. I went along with the tactic because I was feeling pretty good about my answer, and thought I really had him this time. Let him have all the time he wants, I thought; it'll just sink in deeper that our whole Western way of thinking is an illusion, an emperor's-new-clothes thing about believing that you had to have a job and possessions and a degree. When I came back with the eyepieces I was walking the way a cat walks—naturally, without any sense of strain or purpose. I felt free.

He dusted off one of the eyepieces and put it in the telescope. "Listen, Mark. You're not a cat, you're a human being. You can't survive just by catching mice and cleaning yourself with your tongue. You have to cooperate with other people to survive, and cooperating with other human beings is hard. It takes effort. Sometimes you have to worry about what you're doing, or what other people are doing. Otherwise you could end up doing something without thinking and making a foolish mistake, and you might regret it for the rest of your life. If you stopped learning, Mark, your problems wouldn't disappear; they'd get much, much worse."

My sense of freedom started to vanish. "But we're animals, Dad, just like cats! We're like, just as natural as they are! There's no reason we can't live naturally, the way we were meant to live, instead of creating this artificial world of, like, accomplishments and status and laws and money and morality."

My father installed one of the eyepieces and checked the focus. "What makes you think that our world of accomplishments and so on is artificial?" he asked.

"Because it exists only in our minds, not in reality!" I answered with all the conviction I could muster. Essentially I was repeating something I had read in a book by Alan Watts called *So What?*, a book that I found I agreed with perfectly but could never quite explain why to an adult.

"But, Mark, our minds are the product of our brains, and our brains evolved naturally. How can the world we've created with our minds not be natural? Does that mean that art isn't natural? Those Zen masters make art, don't they? I thought I read once that they claim to make their whole lives into art. Doesn't that mean that they're being artificial all day long?"

One thing you could always count on with my dad was that if you sensed you were losing an argument with him and decided to retreat by changing the subject before he could really finish you off, he always let you get away. This meant that he was never able to argue himself into getting a raise or into having his money refunded for faulty merchandise, but it got me out of a lot of tough situations when I was an adolescent. I said I'd get back to him on that and asked if he really thought our telescope had enough light-gathering power to make the faint Horsehead Nebula visible.

"Probably not," he said wearily, displaying another characteristic of his that you could always count on.

Dad had bought the telescope in 1970, thanks to a seren-dipitous accident. While paying the bills one morning my mother realized she had made an error calculating the balance in their checkbook. Over time this error had compounded, leading to an inadvertent savings of eight hundred dollars, a huge amount back then for a social worker, his wife and three children. When the initial excitement died down, my father told my mother that if they didn't apply the money immediately to the principal on their car loan, they could live to regret it terribly one day. My mother, who usually deferred to his judgment when it came to doomsday predictions, firmly disagreed. She insisted that since she had saved the money (inadvertently or not) she could decide how to use it. Half of it could go to the car loan, she decreed, and with the other half my father had to buy himself a telescope.

My father did his best to change her mind, conjuring up an assortment of grim scenarios for our family if we didn't put all eight hundred dollars toward the loan ("Here we are still paying for it, Martha, when it's already rusted out and has already nearly a hundred thousand miles on it—what are we going to do when the engine dies?"), but she outwitted him by leaking word of the telescope plan to Erich, Rachel and me. With us pestering him full-time he didn't stand a chance, and by the end of the weekend he had to admit defeat and agree to treat himself to the one gift he'd wanted all his life.

After weeks and weeks of guilty but careful deliberation—reflector or refractor? high magnification or wide field of view? Newtonian or Cassegrain?—he settled on an F/8 Newtonian reflector with an eight-inch-diameter mirror and an equatorial mount. This means that it was a damn powerful amateur telescope; the tube was nearly six feet long, and with it on a clear day you could read a doctor's eye chart from half a mile away. He ordered it from Criterion Telescopes, a small company in Hartford chosen partly for its good reputation but also for its proximity to us. He could pick up the telescope himself when it was done and thus be assured that every penny of his four hundred dollars went into optics and not into shipping and handling.

Six months passed. When at last the call came, all of us felt a terrific sense of excitement; for as long as I could remember my parents had had to exercise such frugality that I had never seen them treat themselves even to a decent Christmas present. Dad arranged to pick the telescope up on a Saturday morning, and I asked to go with him. That year I was ten years old.

The Criterion telescope company was almost impossible to find. As I recall, it lay in an alley of warehouse buildings with only a yellowed business card taped to a door to identify the entrance. We rang a buzzer and waited in a drizzling rain before someone wearing safety glasses let us in. We passed through a dark, musty room, then got into an elevator that was operated by ropes. On the second floor we stepped over empty telescope tubes and eyepiece housings, past long benches lined with drill presses and clamps, under a series of bare lightbulbs to a spot near a blurry factory-style window. The place looked scary, but I loved the way it smelled: wood shavings, glue, dope-based paints and the irresistible scent of electric tools glistening with oil. It was a little boy's olfactory dream come true.

"Here it is," the technician announced, pointing to two huge boxes, one squat and extremely heavy containing the mount and tracking equipment, and the other over six feet long, which contained the tube with the delicate optics inside. He and another man helped my father get the boxes into the elevator and out to the car. The telescope builders stood in the rain to wave good-bye to us as we drove away; I thought it was because they were sad to see the telescope taken away, but my father said, "Don't kid yourself, those poor guys just don't want to have to go back to work." Once we escaped from downtown Hartford and were at least two highway exits away, we breathed easier, and I, unable to stand the anticipation any longer, climbed back over the front seat, scrambled to the rear of our Volkswagen bus and started clawing at the cardboard boxes to get them open.

When you're ten years old, you don't open big cardboard boxes without cutting your fingers on the heavy staples, and this was no exception. By the time I had the long box open I knew my mother would have a fit when she saw my hands ("You might never play the cello again!"), but I didn't care—I could see the telescope. It was a flawless pearly-white tube with jet-black rims at either end and a blue metal finder scope bolted near the eyepiece hole. It was simply beautiful.

I made my way back to the front seat and babbled for nearly the whole ride home: it's incredible, it's bigger than

I am, we'll be the only people in Connecticut with one of these, we'll probably be able to see the astronauts the next time they walk on the moon with it!

Instead of seeming excited, my father looked even grimmer than usual, and the more I raved about the telescope the worse he looked. I couldn't understand it; he had finally gotten a present, the present of presents, a toy beyond even my wildest fantasies that he'd had to wait thirty years for, and he didn't seem particularly happy about it. During the months we had waited for the telescope I had taken to imagining what it would be like to see my father giddy with pleasure, wringing his hands with the joy of acquisition and running around the house kicking at wads of packing materials and wrapping paper the way we kids acted on our birthdays and Christmas. But it wasn't turning out that way. Frustrated, I asked if he wasn't happy now that at last he had a fancy, expensive telescope. I noticed he winced when I said the word "expensive."

He didn't reply at first, and in the silence the windshield wipers and the engine came to sound deafening. "Well, Mark," he finally said, shaking his head and adjusting his grip on the steering wheel, "I'm afraid I've bitten off more than I can chew."

We looked for the Horsehead Nebula for over an hour but couldn't find it. I was sure it was the light pollution; Dad was sure it was his telescope. To cheer ourselves up we looked at a few old favorites like the Orion Nebula, which looks like a translucent gray jellyfish, and the planet Jupiter surrounded by five of its moons. Astronomers don't get tired of seeing the same objects over and over, partly because these images are so deeply strange

41

and beautiful, but also because each time you see the visual images you are reminded of the immense distances, sizes and energies they represent. For this reason astronomers often say the same things over and over when they go out observing, but there is no embarrassment or sense of cliché about it at all. Whenever my father and I went stargazing, at some point in the evening one of us would say, "It makes you feel small, doesn't it?" And the other would always agree, but this feeling meant something different to him than it did to me. He would back away from the telescope, look upward and say, "We spend most of our lives not even aware that all of that is out there! We all think we're so important, so special, but then you look up and you realize, *Who do we think we're kidding?*" Then he would laugh quietly to himself.

I, on the other hand, liked feeling small because it made my failures insignificant. The gap between who I actually was (a tiny eighth-grader who couldn't impress girls) and who I wanted to be (a perfect kung fu master living in a mist-concealed valley) seemed much smaller under the night sky than it did in any of my school classrooms or in the Circle of Fighting at the Chinese Boxing Institute.

The Circle of Fighting was an area marked off with masking tape on the floor of our kung fu school. Whereas any part of the floor could be used for stretching, drills, forms (choreographed sequences of moves) or weapons exercises, the Circle of Fighting was special; it was where we either got beaten up by Sensei O'Keefe or tried to beat one another up. Since kung fu was an ancient and respected art form invented by nonviolent Buddhist monks, however, we learned that fighting practice was really all about learning respect for others, so we usually stopped short of injuring each other seriously and kept our temper under control most of the time. Actually the circle itself was a square, but the Circle of Fighting has a nicer ring to it than the Square of Fighting, so that's what it was called.

I did not fare well in the Circle of Fighting. I had never participated in a contact sport in my life, much less ever been in a fight, so I had no experience to draw on at all. I was small, terrified of being hit, and far from my goal of being impervious to pain. Because I practiced so much at home my punches and kicks came to look pretty good, and after seeing me shadowbox, most people expected me to be a challenging sparring partner. But after hearing me throw up with anxiety before lessons, then watching me step into the Circle and have my anxieties justified in every conceivable way, these same people often wondered aloud what on earth I was doing in a kung fu school. I loathed sparring, not because I had any moral objection to fighting, but because I was so excruciatingly bad at it. Every time I heard Sensei give out the command, "Bow to me—bow to each other—fight!" I felt my will to master kung fu turn to jelly. I just couldn't be aggressive, and to be any good at all at sparring you must learn to assert yourself. When an opportunity presents itself and your opponent shows an opening or weakness, you have to decide instantly to attack, and you must do so with total commitment. You can't attack halfheartedly, just to see how it goes, and if things look good then follow through. You get hurt that way, for the same reason that a gymnast can't do a backflip at half speed just to make sure it's safe. I never fully grasped this principle, however, so I got hurt a lot and rarely scored any points. But after being punched or kicked, I always managed to recover my balance and strike a good-looking traditional posture.

"He gets the *living shit* kicked out of him every time, but he sure looks good, don't he?" Sensei O'Keefe used to say when he was in a good mood, and everybody would laugh, including me. I much preferred ridicule to the other kind of critique he gave me, which he offered when he was in a bad mood or had been drinking or—which was the usual case—both, and it went something like this: "Listen, candy-ass, do you think if you're jumped by three assholes who don't give a shit whether you live or die that you're gonna live if you fight like that? I don't want to see any more of that *pussy* bullshit, I want you to do what I've been telling you every goddamned lesson, which is: Forget all your fancy book learning and your pretty technique and forget about protecting your pretty little face! All that doesn't mean shit in the street! You live in real life, not some ivory tower! Real life is about life and death, goddammit! You're just another momma's boy smart-ass who thinks he's too good to have to mess with real life, but it's gonna stare you in the face someday, candy-ass, and what are you gonna do about it? When you can't run home to your musical mommy and your *needlepointing* daddy"—my father had once worked on a needlepoint of an Edward Hopper painting while waiting for me in the parking lot of the Boxing Institute—"in your safe little house in the suburbs, huh? I'll tell you what'll happen, candy-ass! You're gonna get ripped to pieces, and you're gonna wonder just before getting your head blown off why somebody didn't prepare you for it. So do yourself a favor and forget about being afraid to get hurt and fight, for Chrissake! There's no room for pussies in this house."

Occasionally, when Sensei O'Keefe decided we needed "a little kick in the ass" to move forward in the arts, he led us through special training exercises, which included a kind of sparring where all the students stood in a circle and each one was assigned a number. One person stood in the center. When Sensei O'Keefe yelled out numbers, each person hearing his number called was to attack the person in the center and keep up the assault until he heard his number called out again. This meant that the person in the center could have as many as five people at a time punching and kicking at him, and if you got too tired to defend yourself, you just got punched and kicked more; no one dared let up because Sensei said that since no one lets up on the streets we had to prepare ourselves accordingly. Sometimes, especially if he'd had too much to drink before the lesson, Sensei would forget which numbers he'd called and it would take forever to clear the Circle. At other times he felt the person in the center wasn't trying hard enough. In that case, Sensei would let out a horrifying scream, jump past the assigned attackers and give the student in the center a beating to remember. When he did that to me one night he hit me so hard on the side of the head that I crashed into a wall and brought a whole shelf of trophies down with me. I sustained a bruise on my temple so deep that it took several days to rise to the surface and form a scab.

Another special exercise was called Cemetery Sparring. We split up into two teams—those with shirts and those without—and left the school separately to hide at opposite ends of a nearby cemetery under cover of night. Practicing our stealth skills, we were to slowly converge on the field of honor and do battle. If we received a decisive blow we had to lie "dead on the field" until the end of the exercise. There was quite a bit of disagreement over what constituted a decisive blow, however, so many of the individual battles went on until one of the parties could in fact do little else but lie on the field. The game ended when one team had been entirely eliminated; then that team had to do one hundred push-ups and run a mile as punishment for losing. Meanwhile, Sensei O'Keefe was a free agent, and wandered around the cemetery on his own to observe or attack as the spirit moved him. The angriest I think I ever saw him was the night he discovered a student hiding in a tree, hoping to survive the game without having to fight at all. That student did not return for lessons, needless to say.

The most reflective I ever saw Sensei O'Keefe was also during one of these cemetery exercises. He had been smoking pot earlier in the evening, which usually made him more subdued than the drinking did. As usual, I was one of the first to die on the field, so I'd had plenty of time to enjoy the crisp fall air and a lovely view of the night sky accompanied by the shouts, smacks and thuds of glorious combat all around me. By the end of the game Bill, the huge man I liked so much, was the only man standing. Just as he prepared to announce that the game was over and we could all stand up, Sensei O'Keefe came flying out from behind a gravestone and, with a bloodcurdling scream, attacked Bill with such ferocity that I thought Sensei might kill him. Bill was not a candy-ass like me, though; he took it all and gave nearly as much back. But exhausted from all his previous battles he finally fell, bleeding from the nose and mouth and with angry red welts rising all over his ribs and back. He went down fighting, and without uttering a single groan or complaint, which explained why Sensei O'Keefe respected Bill more than any of his other students.

Pleased with Bill's example of courage and determination, and perhaps a bit relieved that he had not lost the battle himself, Sensei O'Keefe called us all together for a little talk. We sat cross-legged in a tight circle around a nineteenth-century grave and Sensei said: "Listen up. You're all here because you want to understand the Path of the Warriors who came long before you. You want to know what this is all about; you want to know what kung fu really means. I'll tell you what it's all about. It's not about winning or losing or wearing a brown belt or a black belt—it's about *learning to die well*. If you find yourself cornered in an alley someday and five guys are bearing down on you with baseball bats or shotguns, you might know you don't stand a chance. You might know that you're gonna die, and that there's nothing you can do to stop those bastards from killing you. But you know what a warrior does then? He doesn't give those bastards the satisfaction of seeing him flinch. He doesn't whine or beg for his life; he dives *right the fuck in* and he takes at least one of those sons of bitches with him when he goes down—that's what he does. If you train with that in your head, if you train like your life depends on it, and if you act like *everything you do* might be the last thing you do on earth, then you'll become a master and you'll wear the black belt like me. Otherwise, you'll always be just another bullshit karate student who breaks a couple of boards on weekends, but never really understands what the Path is all about."

We bowed to him and to one another, uttered our little prayer about kung fu being our secret, and then, without having to be told, ran the punitive mile at top speed, shouting one another on and feeling like gods. The winning team was so pumped up that they joined us for the run, and when we returned to the school we did our hun-

47

dred push-ups in the parking lot together, on our bare knuckles on a patch of asphalt covered with broken glass.

That was one of the high points of my experience at the Chinese Boxing Institute, partly because of the seductive mixture of fear, violence and male bonding, but mainly because of Sensei O'Keefe's speech, which had brought me to a realization that I was convinced had to be enlightenment at last: when he said that kung fu was about learning to die well, it occurred to me that this must be what the *Tao Te Ching* meant when it said that one should become like a block of wood. Of course! It meant that you should act as if you were already a dead man and had nothing to lose! That, in turn, explained all the references to emptiness; an empty mind, I deduced, was a mind empty of hope for the future or of petty cares about one's safety, comfort or possessions. That night, at home in the basement, I decided to test the strength of my realization by sitting up all night in the lotus position like the Buddha. I wouldn't budge or relax my concentration until the first rays of sunlight came in through the window—I would sit as if it were my last night on earth before being executed at dawn.

I began my vigil at around 11:00 P.M. By twelve o'clock my back was killing me and I was feeling exhausted. By twelve-fifteen I knew I was going to fall asleep, but I saved the evening by reminding myself that being in a sense already dead, I no longer had to care about proving to myself that I was enlightened or not, so I could do whatever I wanted. Much relieved, I crawled into bed, a kung fu master at last.

My father woke me up at six-thirty; even dead men have to go to school in our achievement-oriented society. I ate

48

some cereal and let him drive me that morning, reasoning that I no longer had to walk barefoot or do anything unpleasant now that I was enlightened. Within an hour my new spiritual status was in trouble, however. I had a crush on a girl in my biology class, so naturally I figured that this would be a good time to ask her out, seeing that I was living in the eternal Now and had nothing to lose. But when the opportunity came to approach her, I froze as usual and she walked right past me, unaware of my inner turmoil. How could I be enlightened and still be nervous about asking someone for a date? I wondered. My temporary solution was to decide that part of being enlightened meant ceasing to make distinctions between behavior that you formerly called "good" or "bad," and accepting that whatever you did was an expression of your inner nature, or your "Original Face before you were born" as the Zen manuals called it. Being insecure was just the way the cosmos decided to manifest itself when I was born.

For two days I dwelt in this state of philosophical limbo, where I still wanted to believe I was enlightened but had to constantly talk myself into ignoring evidence to the contrary. My epiphany came to an end on the third day, when I went back to the Chinese Boxing Institute and got called into the Circle of Fighting. At the sound of my name my knees went weak as usual, I got beat up by my opponent as usual, and then got yelled at by Sensei O'Keefe afterward for being a candy-ass, also as usual. This couldn't be enlightenment, I finally admitted to myself, because none of the Asian philosophy books I had read said anything about enlightenment's being just as miserable as ignorance.

4

Just before entering the ninth grade at school, I persuaded my parents to let me give up my cello lessons. I'd started playing the cello when I was seven, after having already tried the violin and piano without much success. It was hardly surprising that I had shown an early interest in music, since my mother was both a concert pianist and a concert oboist who practiced a minimum of four hours a day, and who gave lessons every afternoon in our living room. She was the first person to major in two instruments at the Eastman School of Music, and was one of the founders of our town orchestra. She loved music, but what really made an impression on me was that she loved practice. Performing was fine, but practice was what it was all about for her, and being able to do it for hours every day meant she was happy for hours a day.

That really burned my dad up. "Don't you ever get tired of playing the same passage over and over and over?" he would ask.

"Of course not! It's different every time! Besides, you know the answer yourself. Don't you love working on your paintings?"

"I like *having painted*, Martha. *Painting* is one big pain in the ass."

"Really? What a shame! I think that's the best part—the struggle!"

My mother was also fond of saying that the neck, back and giblets were the best part of the chicken. She sure was easy to please.

Unfortunately, I took after my father more than my mother when it came to work habits. I hated practice. It was a joyless exercise, made bearable only by the implied promise that if I kept at it, I would eventually become "good" and then people would finally have to take me seriously. I started violin when I was four, and showed some promise. When I was five the music teacher at our school invited me to join the orchestra. When I walked into the music room for my first rehearsal, however, it so happened that the teacher had just stepped out of the room for a moment. That was all the older kids needed to reduce me to tears with their teasing—"Look at the baby! Ha, ha!"—and that was the end of the violin for me.

After that I tried learning the piano from my mother, but every time she criticized me I felt my whole body go rigid with frustration, so that lasted less than a year. Then in 1967 my mother took me to hear Aldo Parisot give a recital of unaccompanied cello pieces. When the concert ended I announced two momentous decisions: I wanted to become a cellist, and I wanted a pair of shoes that were as shiny as Mr. Parisot's.

My cello teacher, Rudolph Gordon, was an exceedingly gentle man who walked with a severe limp, often using his old cello as a cane. Our lessons were in his study, which had a grandfather clock in it that ticked loudly and occasionally threw off my sense of rhythm during lessons. As sweet as he was—I quickly grew very fond of him—I always felt a bit frightened of Mr. Gordon. It had nothing to do with anything he said or did; I was shy and frightened of almost everybody when I was a kid, but teenagers and old people made me particularly nervous. Mr. Gordon's limp, his deep voice and his bald head—added to the fact that I was not a particularly brilliant cello student—all prevented me from ever truly relaxing around him. During one of our lessons I realized I had to use the bathroom, but I could not bring myself to admit it. I don't know what the big deal is for kids about going to the bathroom, but I just kept playing, my mind racing and my bladder in agony. At last I could stand it no longer and wet my pants. I never stopped playing, though. When the lesson ended I stood up, holding the cello in front of me, and walked backward out of Mr. Gordon's house. My shoes made a little *squish-squish* with every step I took. It truly did seem like the end of the world.

After I had spent six years with Mr. Gordon, he modestly recommended that I move on to a more serious teacher and try out for a spot with the Norwalk Youth Symphony, the state's best youth orchestra. I started taking lessons with someone in Westport, an hour's drive away, and every Saturday morning there was another hour's drive to Norwalk for orchestra rehearsal, which lasted two hours.

Once I got into kung fu I found it harder and harder to bring myself to practice the cello, and orchestra rehearsals came to seem unbearable. I brought my Chinese philosophy books to the rehearsals and often had them open on my music stand so I could read them while pretending to be playing. When I asked my parents to let me quit the orchestra, they were disappointed at first, but finally got used to the idea. For my last concert with the orchestra, my grandparents in Ohio drove up to Connecticut to be there. On the first dramatic note of our first piece, I got a little too excited and came down on the string too hard with my bow, which snapped in two. Usually the string breaks, not the bow, but that night it was the bow. I had to sit onstage through the whole piece staring at all the tangled horsehair and hoping my grandparents had a good sense of humor.

Getting out of cello lessons was harder. I had to work on my parents all summer to get that bill passed. By the fall, however, I was free to spend all of my time after school and all weekend meditating and practicing kicks. That was when I knew I had to go the next step and lobby for my own bedroom.

I had shared a tiny room with Erich for thirteen years. This arrangement had worked fine until the time I decided to become a Zen monk, and then a disturbing change came over him. Whereas in the past he would only tease me for doing something especially foolish, his manner now suggested that he thought I was getting weird overall and needed close supervision. He had inherited my father's withering, disapproving gaze, and he started using it on me more and more often. Unlike Dad, however, Erich had a booming voice and charisma to burn, making him difficult to ignore. My sitting in the lotus position on the couch when we watched *All in the Family,* for example, bugged him. He would lean across Rachel (he consistently got her to sit in the middle, where the two cushions never quite met and all the springs below had collapsed, by reminding her that in chess as in life, queens always sit between their servants), flash me that look and say, "I'll bet those guys in China wouldn't sit like that if they could afford chairs." He also didn't like the way I ate pork chops, fish sticks and even corn on the cob with chopsticks. We three kids always ate dinner on this same living-room couch, using fold-up trays so that we could watch television while we ate. Erich would rush to empty his plate, then point to my still-unfinished dinner and say, "If you ate with a fork and knife like a normal person you'd be done by now and we could eat dessert."

Erich had always been a force to contend with. When he was three he fell into a swimming pool while my father's back was turned. After another man fished him out, Erich shook himself off, frowned at Dad and said, "Why don't you take better care of me?" When he was nine he tried to get my mother to quit smoking by stuffing tiny explosive caps into her cigarettes. Now he was twelve and, given that Mom and Dad were apparently letting me slide right off the deep end without a fight, felt saddled with the responsibility of showing me the error of my ways. Incense made the house smell bad, he declared. Only babies and old people walked around in their pajamas during the daytime. Americans drink Lipton's tea, not some kooky stuff that doesn't even come in bags, for God's sake. But his real pet peeve was my meditating. This drove him nuts. "You're *not* thinking of nothing," he would seethe while I sat cross-legged at the foot of our bunk bends. "That's impossible! I'm only in sixth grade and even I know that. You're thinking of something right now. Faker."

Erich conceded that the martial arts aspect was OK, but it enraged him that I wouldn't use it to avenge myself on the assholes who made fun of me for being short and having a high voice. I tried to explain to him that being a kung fu master meant knowing that it was better to walk away from a fight than to hurt someone, but he didn't buy that for a minute. "Couldn't it be," he asked, his eyes narrowing, "that kung fu masters are just a bunch of *chickens*? If *not fighting* is so great, how come they spend their whole lives learning how to break people's jaws? Why don't they just practice letting people beat them up, if being peaceful is so great? God, Mark, that's the stupidest thing I've ever heard." In short, Erich, his booming voice and his common sense posed an unacceptable threat to the unfathomable knowledge of old. I needed privacy.

There weren't any extra rooms in our house, so I proposed that I move down into my basement temple. I already had all of my books and candles and incense down there; all I needed was a clothes hamper and my half of the bunk bed. Eventually Mom and Dad agreed to this, but they reminded me that I would have to share the basement during the daytime with my mother, who had taken out a loan that year and commissioned a harpsichord maker to build an instrument for her so that she would no longer have to borrow or rent one for her early-music performances. When the instrument was ready it would have to go into the basement.

Unlike pianos, which have sturdy metal frames, harpsichords are made almost entirely of wood. Rapid changes in temperature or humidity can make the soundboards warp or crack, causing expensive or even irreparable damage. The basement was the only room in our house whose temperature and humidity were fairly stable and could be regulated easily; it goes without saying that my jumping spinning back kicks, spear thrusts and sword flourishes would have to be regulated as well. Based on what I had done to the walls and ceiling before the arrival of the harpsichord, the new regulation was that I had to take my kung fu outdoors.

The new harpsichord arrived a month later and, along with my clothes dresser and coffee-table shrine, almost filled the basement. To save space, I left my bed upstairs and slept on an old feather couch cushion (a very old cushion, in fact—my father had been born on it) with my head just under the harpsichord. My mother's fierce eagerness to practice, set against my tendency to sleep late on the weekends, led to a morning ritual that I complained about at the time but now think back on with fondness. She would tiptoe down the stairs, presumably so as not to wake me up, sit down as quietly as possible at the harpsichord and then start playing Bach. While it is true that the harpsichord is quieter than the piano, it isn't much quieter, particularly if it is a seven-foot-long French double manual and you are sleeping with your head directly underneath it.

Unbeknownst to my mother, I taped what I considered to be an essential quote from one of my Zen books to the bottom of her instrument so it would be the first thing I saw in the morning and the last thing I saw before going to sleep. The quote read: *"The attainment of enlightenment brings a feeling of unshakable interior peace as well as unequalled security and liberty. The tensions with regard to becoming are absent, and the peace of Being alone remains."*

This message was supposed to inspire me, but after my false-alarm experience with enlightenment, it only served to remind me at least twice a day of my failure. Disgusted with myself, I saw how deeply I was still mired in *becom-*

ing. It would not have been so bad if I was at least *becoming* more popular at school or more self-confident, but the opposite was true. I was no longer "just like a little brother" to my female classmates; I was now "kind of like a weird little brother" to them. It may be hard for people who have grown up listening to bands like Talking Heads and Boy George to imagine a time when weirdness was an obstacle to popularity, but 1974 was just such a time. You could be wild, like Ted Nugent or Ozzy Osbourne, but not weird. If you drank and smoked pot until you passed out, drove a Camaro with slicks on the back wheels and primer sprayed all over the body, set something on fire inside the school building or made noises loud enough to cause adults to have fits, you were wild, but if you cut the soles out of the bottoms of your shoes, read books on your own and meditated in the outdoor smoking lounge, you were weird and pretty much undatable.

In spite of my apprenticeship to a man who referred to himself as an Ass-Kicking Motherfucker, I commanded little respect from the boys in my class. Who cared if I could break bricks or kick three feet higher than my head if I never even argued with anybody? Status among the boys in my school was determined by action, not potential. In any case, athletic prowess held little sway among the members of my class; the few jocks we had were considered out of touch. Success in academics, needless to say, was also a liability, and playing a musical instrument like the cello was hardly something to brag about. Conventional ambitions were looked upon with suspicion. During a school assembly one brave soul dared to get up onstage and sing "The Candy Man" with a few girls dancing around him dressed like dolls and holding giant lollipops. You had to admire him; he really belted it out, gesturing with his hands, doing complicated dance steps and singing with lots of vibrato but no irony. He paid a price for it, however. The whole song was accompanied by a chorus of snickers and guffaws from the audience that became deafening near the end when one boy yelled out, "Show us your candy cane, man!" I don't remember ever seeing the poor candy-man singer again after that morning.

Although I was not by any means the class valedictorian, my interest in Chinese culture indicated an enthusiasm for learning, which was not cool; a cool person did not show enthusiasm, with the single exception of being eager to party at all times. The surest way to earn the affection and respect of one's peers in the mid-seventies, marvelously depicted in the movie *Dazed and Confused* (which I considered a documentary when I saw it), was to provide beer, marijuana or transportation for the parties held every night out in the fields during the summer and on weekends during the school year. Since I was obsessed with purity and feared that alcohol or drugs might weaken my mind, and since I was too young to drive, I occupied a low position in the class hierarchy. Occasionally I won points by being funny in school, but class clowns are never truly popular because the very reason anyone pays attention to them is also the reason no one takes them seriously. And I, who willingly submitted to all sorts of physical and mental punishment in order to learn how to "die well," wanted more than anything in the world to be taken seriously.

Even worse than my failure to become more popular at school, however, was the growing realization that instead of making me different from my father by producing total inner fulfillment, my struggle was in fact making me more and more like my father: perpetually disappointed. But I felt stuck. As I saw it, if I dropped the whole matter I would piss most of my life away like Scrooge, never questioning or understanding what I did or why I did it, chasing illusions like money and power only to realize just before the end of my life that they all had slipped through my fingers. On the other hand, if I kept pining after the experience of feeling no need to pine after anything, what if I never got it right and wasted my whole life making myself purposely uncomfortable? Or what if I woke up twenty or thirty years down the road and realized that my father had been right to be skeptical of my attempt to become like a block of wood? What if Zen itself was an illusion created by unhappy people who had invested too much of themselves in their "spiritual path" to consider that enlightenment might be a hallucination?

I couldn't admit the most serious of these doubts to my father because that would have seemed like a defeat, and I wasn't yet defeated. I did mention to him on one of our weekend trips to the town dump, however, that I was disappointed with my progress with kung fu. We were watching a bunch of crows maneuver around a bulldozer as it pushed some fresh garbage, and I said I didn't understand why, if crows could eat garbage and not seem particularly unhappy with their lot, it bothered me so much to be such a coward compared with, say, Sensei O'Keefe. I told him about Sensei's example of dying well by facing one's enemies bravely even under impossible circumstances and fighting without being hampered by indecision or fear.

"Mark," he said, wincing as if all of a sudden he had noticed that the dump smelled bad, "that is *ridiculous*."

I was shocked; he was usually more careful in his choice

of words when offering criticism. "What do you mean, *ridiculous*? Why is it ridiculous?"

"Because it's a fantasy. It's fine to enjoy as a fantasy, but it's silly to get it mixed up with real life. I don't care how long you study karate, Mark—you want to know what would really happen if you found yourself in an alley cornered by a dozen men with weapons who were about to kill you?"

"What?"

He looked right at me. "You'd shit your pants. And so would I. So would any normal human being. Trying to make yourself immune to things like fear is *dumb*, because there are perfectly good reasons to be afraid of dangerous situations. All living things with brains have evolved to feel fear—it's for self-protection, it has nothing to do with your being a weakling. Just be yourself, Mark. You'll do just fine as you are."

Be yourself! What a can of worms he opened there. Of course I was trying to be myself! That was the whole point of the kung fu; to become the me I thought I ought to become, instead of some half-assed loser. Anyway, who was to say who I really was? I didn't even know *that*— that was half my problem right there. All I knew was that when you're a really little kid, your parents praise you when you do something they like. If you do something they don't like, they say, "You're not the sort of person who does that! Don't try to be somebody you're not! Be yourself!" So maybe, I reasoned, being yourself means being the person your parents or teachers want you to be. Do we have anything to do with who we are at all? As we get older, we think of ourselves as having unique personalities, and we take credit for these personalities when we do something good, as if we created these personalities ourselves. But maybe we didn't! Maybe our personalities were shaped by how people around us responded to us. So who are we? As I said, this was a can of worms I didn't care to dip into—at least not that day.

I stuck to a more immediate issue: no matter how hard I tried, I could not picture Sensei O'Keefe or Bruce Lee shitting their pants in the face of danger, and so I was not yet willing to picture myself doing it either. I asked my father how he could be so sure that a two-thousand-year-old tradition that had produced generations of enlightened masters was wrong.

"I'm not saying it's wrong, Mark. I'm just saying that because you're *not* a guy living in medieval China I don't think you should kick yourself for not being exactly like those people. I think it's good that you think so much about these things, but don't be crushed if they don't turn out the way you want them to. Lots of things don't work out the way you want them to, regardless of how good your intentions are. It's disappointing, but you do learn to live with it."

Well, I already knew that my father was able to live with disappointment. He proved every day that it was possible to survive in an uncaring, purposeless universe without becoming evil or alcoholic, and I respected that; it was just that I hoped to do better. Instead of just surviving, I aspired to go through life feeling as if every moment and every experience were precious. There had to be a way of looking at things so that even if they didn't turn out the way one expected them to, they still appeared to be turning out great. My dad gave in to resignation too easily, I thought.

. . .

Although his resignation did not make my father a glamorous role model for a teenage boy, it made him an excellent amateur astronomer. You must possess a high tolerance for disappointment to maintain an interest in objects and events so dramatically beyond your control, not to mention so dramatically beyond your reach. For example, every August on the night of the Perseid meteor shower, when the earth passes through a band of the solar system unusually crowded with bits of rock and dust, my father set up a cot in the front yard and hoped for good weather. If the skies were clear he brewed a pot of coffee, lay out on the cot and stayed up all night to watch the falling stars, hoping to witness one of those extremely rare peaks of activity called a meteor storm. This occurs when the earth hits a particularly "dusty" section of space and runs into as many as several tens of thousands of meteors in an hour, each one making a bright streak across the sky as it burns up in our atmosphere. Astronomers estimated that during the most famous meteor storm of all, the Leonid Storm of November 1833, some 260,000 meteors fell into the atmosphere over a period of twenty-four hours. At times they counted as many as twenty falling each second. One Native American chief out in the Midwestern plains saw it and depicted the event in a painting on the outside of his teepee, which was preserved and can still be seen today in the Smithsonian Museum. Witnesses of these storms say that it is like driving through a blizzard at night, and that it is the only time a person can actually sense the earth's movement as it hurtles through space at nearly seventy thousand miles per hour. Despite his perseverance over the years, my father has never seen a meteor storm. One did occur in the early

1960s, but that year the skies over Connecticut were overcast.

All sorts of things can frustrate an astronomer's attempts to observe a rare event or a particularly distant object. Even one's own personality can get in the way. In 1970 my dad drove Erich and me down the coast to Norfolk, Virginia, to see the most spectacular of all astronomical events visible with the naked eye: a total eclipse of the sun. He had planned the trip several years in advance, the last three months of which he spent poring over maps of the eastern United States, even though Interstate 95 took us the whole way. He had three cameras ready, two hand-held and the other fixed on a tripod, and led Erich and me through several practice sessions where we choreographed what stages of the eclipse to watch out for, who would be in charge of what camera, and what to do in case one of them jammed.

At last the time came. Dad woke us up at 1:00 A.M., tucked us into the back of the Volkswagen bus, and we drove all night. Erich and I tried to prove how big we were by staying awake, but by the time we reached Rye, New York, we were both snoring. I do remember waking up at about 4:00 A.M. when Dad stopped for gas and got his thermos filled with coffee. The smell of coffee in the middle of the night in a car on a highway, somewhere in a part of the country I'd never been to before, made me feel like one of the astronauts on his way to the moon.

We drove and drove; we saw the sun come up in Maryland, and arrived at Cape Charles beach at around ten-thirty. We had a few hours to kill, so Erich and I paced up and down the beach, collecting crab claws for Rachel and poking at a huge dead seagull with sticks. We waited and waited for so long that I lost track of what exactly it was we were waiting for. Dad had us look through strips of exposed film at the sun, and we could see that its image was now in the shape of a crescent. The moon really was there, and at least it was on track. Still, as soon as you took away the strip of film, the sunlight seemed just as bright as always, and the world didn't look changed at all. Erich and I were getting impatient; so far this was not worth the drive.

But then it seemed that at a certain point the world got dusky. It was as if a soft, brownish dye had been added to the atmosphere. My father began to get focused and told us to get ready. Ten long minutes passed; then he pointed out over the ocean and said, "Here it comes."

During a total eclipse the moon blocks out the sun entirely, casting a perfectly round shadow on the earth. Since the earth spins on its axis toward the east, the shadow always moves west; because we were standing on the Atlantic coast, the shadow raced over the water directly toward us, allowing us to see it from quite a distance. It was a distinct wall of darkness that spanned the horizon, and it was moving *fast*. When it reached us, everything changed without a sound.

The whole sky went ultramarine, the color that appears in every child's paint set, and which every child uses to depict the sky. No sky is ever really that blue, however, until you see an eclipse, and then it really *is* that blue. The color was so rich and deep that the stars shone through it, while the horizon glowed a luminous red. The air had been full of noisy seagulls, but when the shadow hit they went silent and dropped like stones into the water. I looked upward and saw, right in the middle of the sky, an indescribably lovely soft white glow. Right in the center of it was a perfect coal-black disk, the image of the moon in front of the sun. It was one of those rare occasions when reality becomes so absurdly unreal that you feel as if you are watching a movie, and worry that you aren't truly grasping the experience while it is happening.

It was the moment of a lifetime. I snapped a few pictures and turned to make sure my father was taking pictures with the big camera, only to see him frantically trying to communicate something to a group of European tourists standing a few yards away from us. After all his planning and staring at Rand McNally maps he wasn't looking at the eclipse; he was trying to get someone *else* to look at it. At the instant of totality, they had all turned around to face the wrong way! Somebody had obviously told them that if you look at an eclipse it will hurt your eyes, which is only true of partial eclipses; during a total eclipse the harmful rays of the sun are blocked, and you're treated to one of the greatest spectacles on earth. Dad was pleading with them to turn around, trying to explain why it was safe, but they didn't understand English and looked as if they thought he was some kind of maniac. Eventually they got angry, clopped off in their strange-looking sandals, got into their rental car and drove off without ever looking up.

The eclipse was spectacular, but I don't think I would remember it so clearly if it hadn't been for that hapless group. The fact that they had made the trip to the beach to see the eclipse and then didn't dare look at it made the sight of that velvet-black disk seem especially rare and beautiful. It also provided me with a memorable image of my father. Totality during that eclipse lasted just over two minutes, and he spent fully half of that time trying to get a bunch of strangers to enjoy it. I suppose it revealed something about my own odd sense of priorities that I felt obliged to spend that whole minute watching him miss the damn thing.

No sooner did we make it back to Connecticut than my father began preparing for our next trip. This time the whole family would go. The next total eclipse visible in North America was predicted to occur two years later, in July 1972; after that, the eclipses for the next century would all occur in places like Africa, the Indian Ocean or the Arctic Circle—out of range for us and our Volkswagen—so a sense of finality hung over this adventure from the start.

Dad calculated that the best place to see the eclipse would be Cap Chat, a town, once again on the water, on the Gaspé Peninsula in northeastern Canada. Our route this time was more complicated, involved several highways and even some local roads, so Dad began examining his maps over a year in advance.

We put a tent on top of the Volkswagen and camped our way north, finally reaching Cap Chat late one morning and having to ask a chain-smoking, French-speaking twelve-year-old to direct us to a spot where we could pitch our tent. We settled on a site in a large, barren field on the outskirts of town. By the next morning we were surrounded by hundreds of tents, each one with a fabulous camera, telescope or other type of instrument perched in front of it. This was a scene entirely different from the one in Virginia. There were no hapless tourists anywhere, but instead hundreds of professional and serious amateur astronomers from all over the world. I had never seen such a variety of technology or heard such a variety of languages.

The third day was the day of the eclipse. At six that

morning we woke up to blue skies. There was only one small cloud on the horizon, so small and distant that most people ignored it, but not my dad. He squinted at it for a long time. Finally he shook his head and said quietly, "It's going to kill us." He crawled back into the tent looking defeated, which seemed awfully premature.

By noon that cloud was a lot closer to the sun, it looked bigger, and it was no longer alone. People around us were beginning to get nervous, but by no means did the situation seem hopeless.

At three o'clock the clouds joined and covered the whole sky, and from 4:32 to 4:34 all we knew was that it got dark out. It looked like the end of any ordinary cloudy day. Several of the astronomers around us were so frustrated they cried; one tore at his hair, kicked the wheels of his car and shouted things I had heard only once before, when I was ten years old, had my brother and sister on my lap in the car and tried to scare them by opening the passenger door while Dad was driving.

My father, on the other hand, was entirely under control. He had already dealt with the loss by lying quietly in the tent by himself before the disaster actually occurred, so while many of the other astronomers were just beginning to realize what had happened and were only now writhing in agony, my father was already figuring out our route back to the main highway. He emerged from the tent and began pulling up its stakes so that we could be on the road before dinner. It occurred to me then, with so many heartbroken grown men around me to compare him with, that he was unusual in the way he dealt with disappointment. I thought, What an effort it must take for him to spare us the sight of him rolling around on the ground and pounding the earth with his fists, as one astro-photographer camped next to us was doing. I realized that this was the first opportunity of my life to reverse our roles—to act like a man and console him the way he had always done for me when I was disappointed. I prepared as much of a speech as any twelve-year-old can compose in his head in a hurry and approached him.

Just before I reached him, however, Dad stood up stiffly and started touching his mouth with one of his hands. He turned toward me and I saw a puzzled expression in his eyes. When he moved his hand away, I saw that both his lips were bright purple and swollen to comic-book proportions. We both stood there, too confused to say anything, when a woman, whose lips were also swollen, walked over and said, "Don't worry—it's a kind of spider that lives around here. My husband got bit this morning, too. The swelling goes down in about an hour."

I'm sure it was Erich who started giggling first. He was always the one who started things. Rachel and even my mother got into it, and before I knew it I was laughing harder than any of them. The puzzlement faded out of Dad's expression and turned to annoyance, and he finished pulling up the tent stakes without a word. That doomed eclipse was the only time nature gave me a text-book opportunity, plump with symbolic as well as concrete value, to become a man right before my father's eyes. Unfortunately, what nature giveth, nature also taketh away: the spider got to my father before I did.

So when Dad told me at the town dump that I had to get used to things not working out in my favor, I was prepared to agree with him, but how does one get used to disappointment? I'd already tried, without success, to get used to physical pain by making myself feel it a lot; setting myself up for disappointment on purpose as a means of building up a tolerance for it probably wouldn't work either. I imagined that a Zen master would say that the root of all disappointment is expectation, and that all expectations are illusions. If one could accept the present moment as it was and let go of the need to control the future, disappointment wouldn't have anything to hang on to. Like all of my Zen insights, however, the idea of letting go of the need to control the future sounded great but I had no idea how to put it into practice. Accept the present moment—immaturity, unpopularity, anxiety, celibacy—and let go of the desire to become an adult, have good friends, discover a way of life I could enjoy and find out, at last, why the French call an orgasm "the small death"? Not bloody likely.

My dad's approach seemed to lie somewhere between a Zen master's ("Come to think of it, this broken leg allows me to experience a new kind of physical sensation, and presents new challenges for mobility!") and my own ("That's *it*; if my life doesn't get better RIGHT NOW, I'm going to shut down entirely and spend the rest of my life letting EVERYBODY ON EARTH know what a shithole the world really is"). My dad hoped for the best, but when the worst started to happen instead, he rarely struggled against it. He would stare right at that flat tire, repair estimate or threatening cloud and stand very still while the frustration first appeared as a little dot between his eyes, then spread like india ink through tissue paper, meeting no resistance at all. He could stand still only because he knew that the frustration would eventually spread thin enough to fade away, and it was best to just get the whole process over with as soon as possible. If you clung too desperately to the hope that you could turn things around, you would merely prolong the suffering (making it all the more painful when you finally did give up)—or worse, become pathetic, like obviously guilty criminals who insist on their innocence long past the time when such protestations can do them any good.

At that time I felt that Dad's policy of nonresistance toward fate, though it had certain virtues, also had one major unacceptable weakness: if a golden opportunity to turn his life into his dreams come true ever *did* present itself, he would not recognize it for what it was because it would undoubtedly come to him heavily disguised as possible misfortune. Every teenager knows that great victories, intellectual or otherwise, only come after great sacrifices and risks. In fact, teenagers know this better than any adult; when we are between the ages of thirteen and twenty-one, we are biologically designed to wonder how anyone could possibly choose the road of moderation and stability, with its unavoidably bland scenery, over the risky but incomparably superior path of taking things to extremes. Because we know which path is superior—every biography ever written tells us so—we cannot imagine that we could ever suffer consequences that would make us regret trying to break on through to the other side. Bad things undoubtedly happened to some of us along the way, but they would always happen to other, stupider, weaker people. The classic example, of course, is that every teenager drives recklessly on occasion. He knows that the faster he drives, the higher his chances of being in an accident, but he is also completely confident that he won't have an accident because he honestly believes the statistics will be fed by some other kid, some idiot with bad reflexes, a bad sense of timing or some as-yet-undetermined flaw.

As you get older your perspective changes. It's not that you want to avoid risk altogether; it's that your sense of being connected to other people and even objects expands over the years, so that you feel you have more to lose; the risks come to seem riskier, while the potential gains come to represent less and less of a dramatic improvement over what you already have. Until you *do* get older, though, you crave drama, and your metabolism practically guarantees that you'll create some. All I could think of when my dad told me to get used to things like not being able to "die well" was, if instead of going into the tent at the sight of that cloud he had jumped into the car and raced up the coast at ninety miles an hour instead of his chronic fifty-five, he might have found a patch of clear sky and seen that eclipse, and think of how different his life would be today! Why couldn't he see that?

I had tried and failed to become enlightened, and knew somehow that my days in the lotus position were behind me, but that didn't mean I had to abandon my quest for perfect happiness, I just had to try a new approach. Just after entering the ninth grade I made a new friend, and he provided me with that new approach.

5

No longer able to practice kung fu in the basement, and wanting more privacy than the front yard could afford, I settled on a clearing in the woods a mile from our house. It was perfect: a patch of hard, level ground next to a small lake with no road access, so I almost always had it to myself. One afternoon, as I was practicing the Three Tiger Forms—shadowboxing routines that include a special kind of punch known as the tiger's claw, a blow with the open palm followed by a downward tearing motion with the fingers—a boy my age appeared out of the woods and marched purposefully toward me. As he got closer, I saw that it was Michael Dempsey, the most feared boy in our school, whose father had died when he was very young and who had been trained since infancy in the arts of helmetless tackle football, blackjack, boxing, Greco-Roman wrestling, broomstick fencing, archery and darts by his four older brothers.

He had learned to drive by the age of five (on a power mower), knew how to aim a Roman candle by the age of seven and had broken both his legs when he was eight trying to pole-vault over a picnic table, lengthwise, using a five-foot length of copper pipe as a pole. His pedigree was phenomenal; by the time he entered the public school system, his four older brothers had already achieved mythical status in our town. Each one had proved himself, through exploits both famous and infamous, to be daring, resourceful and virtually indestructible. Together, the brothers were described variously as the Immortals, the Golden Horde (the name of the Mongol army at its peak) and, as once overheard at a Beer Garden event, Hell's Eagle Scouts.

For many years I, along with many of the other boys in our elementary school, thought that the Dempsey brothers ate human flesh for strength and drank gasoline for stamina. I had been told that the three older brothers once kidnapped a kid who had been rude to their mother (she worked in the school cafeteria and everyone loved her), drove him out of state in the trunk of a car, stripped him naked, shaved his head and left him to walk home. Another story went that a high school dropout boy with no parents at all went to their house for a keg party and tackle-football game, during which he purposely tripped either the number two or number three Dempsey brother (this varied according to who was telling the story), was invited to have a look at their basement later that day and was never seen again.

I had spent a large part of my elementary school recess time either running away from Michael Dempsey or trying to prove myself worthy of being a member of his gang, the Ebers (a name he'd made up whose meaning was never revealed to me), rather than its favorite target. As early as 1968 my position with him was shaky. That year one of our teachers tried to encourage us to participate in democracy by having us choose a presidential candidate—Nixon or Humphrey—learn about him and then support him in a class debate planned for the morning before the election. I had chosen Humphrey and Michael had chosen Nixon, and it so happened that we were assigned to be debating opponents. I gave my little speech first, but when it came Michael's turn his face reddened and he said, "I, uh . . . thought we were supposed to do this tomorrow," leading the teacher to scold him in front of the class for not taking important tasks seriously. I was dead meat. Sure enough, at recess he enlisted the help of all the other preadolescent Republicans, dragged me out to the woods, tied me to a tree and wrapped me from head to toe in Nixon bumper stickers.

In the fifth grade Michael went through a gunpowder phase, grinding huge quantities of it with a mortar and pestle taken from one of his brothers' chemistry sets. He was forever lighting piles of it in the school parking lot and showing everyone how the intense heat could actually melt asphalt or even concrete. Inevitably he came up with a more ambitious project, though: he announced his intention of making a large bomb. He needed a proper vessel, so I, hoping to ingratiate myself with him, gave him my old GI Joe doll. Michael accepted the offering and eagerly stuffed it from head to toe with his homemade powder. Then he drilled a small hole in the top of Joe's head, put a fuse through it, and told everyone to meet him in the cattail swamp at the edge of the school playing fields.

Michael stood the doll up against a piece of driftwood and lit the fuse, then ran over to where the rest of us were crouched behind a large rock. The fuse hissed and sputtered; then the lit part of it disappeared into GI Joe's head. There was a pause, and we all started to say "Awww!" thinking that the bomb was a failure, when all of a sudden a flash of light appeared over Joe's head. In an instant the flash became a tremendous violent flame at least four feet high; instead of blowing up, GI Joe became something of an upside-down rocket, with his head acting as the nozzle. The intense heat seemed to act on the plastic all at once, and his standing figure melted instantly, like the Wicked Witch, leaving nothing but a huge cloud of white smoke and a pile of frantically bubbling sulfur on the ground. Everyone was laughing except Michael, who was once again red in the face with anger. The last thing I remember was his punching me in the stomach for ruining his bomb.

Later that year Michael went through a BB-gun phase. Every boy in our school had a BB gun, and every boy had promised his parents never to point his gun at a living thing, but of course in no time every boy was pointing his gun at birds and squirrels. It was Michael, however, who had the revolutionary idea of using the guns to shoot at other kids. It began with a game called Execute the Prisoner. I, along with two other boys who were also not Ebers, was the prisoner; Michael was always the executioner. As prisoner, you stood next to the executioner, and at a signal from a third person, you started to run as fast as you could. The executioner was supposed to count to five before pumping up his rifle and shooting you in the back.

This worked OK for a while; the distance you gained by running meant that when the BB hit you, it burned as if you'd been stung by a wasp and left a welt, but was bearable. Unfortunately, Michael was the sort of person who got bored easily. One day we were playing Execute the Prisoner and he managed to pump up his gun beforehand without anyone's noticing. When the signal was given and poor Donald—thankfully, it wasn't me that time—started to run, Michael instantly lowered the rifle and shot, hitting Donald in the back of the thigh. Michael was delighted with the results, but Donald was not—he never played with us again—so it was decided that in order to always have a fresh supply of prisoners, we had to make the game more fair. That was when Michael, who loved all things related to battle, opened his eyes wide and said, "BB-gun wars! Why didn't I think of it before!"

Michael was a bit of troublemaker, but he was a creative and, thanks to the examples set by his older brothers, a highly organized troublemaker. He loved regulations and strategies. Over the next week he worked out the rules of combat (which he adapted from his favorite board games *The Battle of Britain*, *Dunkirk* and *Sink the Bismarck*), scouted a perfect location, drew a detailed map of it and worked out a battle plan for how he and his Allied Forces could surround and crush their enemies. To my dismay, when the time came for picking teams, I was assigned to the Axis army.

Michael had chosen the Allied and Axis teams not on the basis of any aptitude any of us might have for leadership, running speed or stealth, but according to how strong our BB guns were. The Allies had the good guns, operated either by pump action or, in one case, a CO_2 cartridge semiautomatic, whereas the Axis powers wielded "My Very First BB Gun" Daisy spring-type rifles—in other words, pieces of shit. If I was lucky enough to hit one of the Allied soldiers, my BB would bounce off his nylon windbreaker without even raising a welt. When one of the Allies hit one of us, on the other hand, every-body knew it from the sound of our wretched squealing.

We held these war games on weekends, usually six boys to a team. Our most serious mishap occurred when one boy attempted a daring flanking attack by sneaking across an ice-covered lake behind enemy lines. Peeking over the wall of our fort, we watched him as he moved stealthily across the lake in a half crouch. One moment he was there, the next moment we heard a crack, a splash, and he was gone. He managed to get himself out of the water, but lost his gun and nearly froze to death when his captors insisted that he stay locked in "prisoner-of-war camp"—an abandoned Chevy Nova—until the battle was over. That was when I first discovered that people really did turn blue when they were cold.

Fortunately, before any of us lost an eye or worse, the commander in chief of the Allies developed a new interest. One of his brothers had brought home a .22 pistol, and that was where the rest of us bowed out. I saw Michael only once during this phase of his development; the Golden Horde had found an abandoned station wagon and driven it out to one of the lakes for an adventure. I'd heard about it beforehand at school—most Dempsey events were publicized well in advance—and got to the lake just in time to see them driving the station wagon, by now shot full of holes, at full speed over ditches and into boulders. In a rare display of concern for safety, they were all wearing football helmets. The finale came when they got out of the car, pointed it at the lake, placed a cinder block on the gas pedal and jammed it into gear. To this day, fishermen get their hooks stuck on its submerged body.

My next series of encounters with Michael occurred in

the sixth grade, when I heard that he and his brothers were building gas-engined model airplanes and solid-fuel model rockets and sending them off into space from their back porch. Once again, hoping to become friendly with Michael, I made a sacrifice: I persuaded my parents to buy me a small model rocket, which I worked on for several days. When the last fin had been glued on and the last decal had dried, I took it over to Dempsey headquarters, and sure enough, three of his brothers and a whole bunch of older boys were spread out on the grass in lawn chairs, drinking beer from a keg and using an electric launchpad to send the rockets up. I handed my rocket to Michael and he laughed. "This dinky thing? Come on, let's give it to Frank. He'll customize it." He banged on the door of the garage, and when it opened there stood the fourth Dempsey brother, Frank, who had long black hair and a Zapata-style mustache, and who could bench-press over three hundred pounds. He must have been sixteen at the time. Frank was the brother who could tell you from memory virtually anything about any major European battle occurring within the last thousand years. Michael handed him the rocket and I swelled with pride. It was my first personal audience with one of the Immortals; I felt like a buck private having his rifle examined by General Patton. Frank looked at my rocket solemnly, ran his fingers over his mustache and finally said, "This'll never reach Berlin, gentlemen. The free world hangs in the balance—we must act immediately."

He led us through their garage and into a dark room known as the Laboratory, which held his weight-lifting equipment and explosives. He put my rocket on the workbench and pulled its solid-fuel engine out from the tube. "Mr. Von Braun doesn't use these, you can be sure of that," he said, tossing the tiny engine into a wastebasket. The man at the hobby shop who sold it to me had said it was the largest engine designed for that scale rocket. Frank opened up a wooden chest filled with rocket engines, gas-powered model engines, fireworks, M80s (quarter sticks of dynamite) and a few unspecified devices rigged with underwater fuses. Pulling out a huge rocket engine identified as Big Bertha, he attempted to insert it into my rocket but without success. "This will require a minor technical adjustment," he said, grinning. He clamped my rocket to the desk and used a pair of heavy shears to slit open the bottom. He managed to stuff the huge engine inside, wrapped black electrical tape around the rocket to firm everything up, and then took it out to the launchpad.

The rest of the Golden Horde and their foot soldiers were sitting around the keg with no shirts on and big plastic cups full of brew propped on the grass next to them. "This is strictly experimental," Frank announced. "Everybody behind the ramparts." He was referring to a pile of old tires and garbage cans set up near the porch. Once everyone had found proper cover, Frank handed me the electrical switch that would ignite my rocket. "The young lieutenant will have the honor of sending his rocket into space," he said with dignified gravity. There was one thing about the Dempsey brothers that you had to admire: they all had a terrific sense of ceremony.

"You mean blowing it to smithereens," someone yelled out from behind the ramparts, but Frank didn't crack a smile.

"Give us a countdown, Lieutenant," he advised me, then took his place behind a car.

I counted down and pressed the button. A huge flame

shot out of the rocket—not unlike what had happened to GI Joe a year earlier—and the rocket blasted off the pad, but then, in a curlicue of smoke and fire about ten feet in diameter, hooked right over, dived into the ground and exploded.

"Heeeeehah!" the D brothers and their friends yelled, clinking their beer mugs together in a grand toast and moving back to their lawn chairs. I was walking over to the smoking hole in the ground that had only moments before been a carefully painted rocket when Michael rushed up alongside me, patted me on the back and said, "It's too bad about that, but it was death with honor! Honor was maintained, even to the ultimate sacrifice!" Glad that for a change he was patting me on the back instead of punching me in the stomach, I decided the loss of the rocket was worth it.

At last I had won Michael's approval, but was not able to enjoy it for long. Two days after the sacrifice of my rocket I rode my bicycle to his house and sat out on the back porch with him while he blew up a model tank submerged in an inflatable swimming pool. So that was what the underwater-fuse devices were for. Suddenly an older boy, with a shock of white hair and freckles, whom I had never seen before got on my bicycle without a word and started playing roughly with the gear lever. "He's wrecking your bike," Michael said. Realizing that I had to act or lose my new status as someone worthy of his company, I called out to the older boy, "Hey, cut it out!"

The boy stopped fiddling with the gears, sized me up and laughed out loud. "Big talk, little man," he said, and, as if to show me how unimpressed he was, started moving the gears even more roughly than before. Against all better judgment, but emboldened by my new alliance with

the youngest member of the Immortals, I shouted after
him, "Big man, little talk!" I turned and smiled nervously
at Michael, hoping he would be pleased, but he was pointing behind me. Before I could turn around I felt myself
being lifted by the collar and being spun around. The
older boy held me in the air for a few seconds, put his face
right up against mine and said, "That was a big mistake,
punk." Then he threw me off the porch.

I landed on my arm with a loud crack. The boy jumped
down, grabbed my busted arm and started twisting it to
make sure I got the message. I think my screaming must
have taken him by surprise, because as I recall he departed
pretty quickly. The result was that I had to wear a cast for
six weeks and Michael lost all interest in me because I
obviously had to be some kind of idiot not to know the
first rule of preteen suburban anarchy: Never provoke
people who are bigger than you.

Given this background, it should come as no surprise that
I viewed Michael's appearance at my lakeside practice site
as a stroke of misfortune. I expected him to challenge me
to a fight instantly; I was on his turf displaying combat
skills, so what else could I expect? Instead his eyes nar-
rowed to slits and he asked, "You know karate?"

"Oh . . . um . . . Actually it's kung fu."

"Yeah? Where'd you learn that?"

"A place called the Chinese Boxing Institute."

Michael's face registered interest mixed with skepti-
cism. "You study with Sensei O'Keefe?" he asked.

"Yeah." How did he know about Sensei O'Keefe? The
Chinese Boxing Institute was three towns away.

"Lemme see some kicks."

I did my best series of front, side, roundhouse and

jumping spinning back kicks, and to my surprise and delight Michael looked impressed.

"One of my brothers took lessons with that guy for a couple of months," Michael said, still eyeing me suspiciously. "He quit, though. He said he didn't feel like getting killed. O'Keefe killed some guy in a fight, you know. He had to do time for it."

I couldn't believe it: *I was learning kung fu from a man who had intimidated one of the Dempsey brothers!* Instead of shocking or worrying me, the news that Sensei might indeed have killed someone only added to my sense of having suddenly become very powerful. It was intoxicating beyond my wildest dreams.

Michael asked to see some of the forms. I noticed as I was going through the routines that instead of being nervous when he watched me, I felt as if a few thousand watts of power had just been allocated to me through the soles of my feet. I had never done the forms so well. Michael, his jaw set with determination, announced that he was going to start lessons right away.

Two days later Michael came with me for his first lesson at the Institute. After he had filled out the required forms, I led him into the office to introduce him to Sensei O'Keefe. The Master looked over the paperwork with a bored expression on his face and gave Michael a receipt for his check. Just as we turned to leave he asked, "So how's your brother?"

"Fine," Michael answered, visibly stiffening. It was hard being the smallest Immortal; no matter where he went, he found himself in the shadow of giants.

"Good fighter. Tell him I said hello," the Master said,

and that was that. Michael looked annoyed, but it was a far more propitious beginning than mine had been.

In the dressing room Michael put on his brother's oversized, faded black karate uniform and tied a red bandanna on his head to keep his hair out of his eyes. One of the men who had made fun of my eggplant costume several months before took a look at Michael's raggedy outfit and said, "Check this out—it's Long John Silver! Where's the eyepatch, pirate?"

Michael said nothing, but I noticed a certain glazed expression come into his eyes. It made them look empty, like a shark's. He didn't take to teasing as well as I did.

After we had done our punching and kicking drills, we moved directly to the Circle of Fighting. I'd had to wait several weeks before being allowed to spar, but Sensei, who was a keen judge of character, sensed that Michael was ripe for combat. After a few lackluster matches, including mine, where, as usual, I got knocked right out of the Circle at least three times, Michael was called on. His assigned opponent was the man who had teased him about his bandanna; Sensei O'Keefe, who I could have sworn was grinning underneath his mustache, truly seemed to know everything.

Michael didn't do much at the beginning except block; he seemed unsure of how to proceed. This was his first day at the school, inevitably he was going to be compared with one of his brothers again, and he was facing a grown man who had been studying kung fu for several years. O'Keefe got impatient quickly: "Come on, Dempsey, don't fuck around. We don't need the humility act. *Fight,* for Chrissake."

Magic words. *You'll remember this bandanna,* Michael

seemed to be thinking as he flung himself at the surprised older man. It was like seeing a mongoose attack a bear, where the mongoose apparently has no idea, or just doesn't care, that he doesn't stand a chance. He punched and kicked at the man with heroic savagery, and nearly backed him out of the Circle, but his opponent got over his surprise in time to gather his wits and get very annoyed. All pretense to giving the kid a break dropped, and he gave Michael a terrible beating, but a Dempsey never gives up. He kept rushing at the man, only to get kicked in the ribs, punched in the face or shoved backward. At last the man did a foot sweep that sent Michael flying through the air and landing hard on his elbow, on a thin rug stretched over a concrete floor. When he stood up he was clutching the elbow and wincing.

"Keep fighting!" O'Keefe yelled. He had a look on his face so intense that it could have melted steel.

"I can't move my arm," Michael said.

"Use the other, then!" O'Keefe shot back, and Michael obeyed instantly. Out of breath and with tears streaming from his eyes, he kept yelling and charging at the man only to be repulsed with a flurry of blows. His elbow was so swollen that it looked as if a tennis ball had been sewn under the skin. At last Sensei boomed, "All right! Bow to me! Bow to each other!" With that ritual out of the way, he told Michael to go clean himself up and get some ice out of the freezer to put on his elbow.

When Michael was out of earshot, Sensei grinned at his surprised opponent, who was visibly relieved that the mongoose had been called off. "Tough little motherfucker, huh?" O'Keefe asked, laughing. Then he grew serious, pointed toward the changing room and frowned at the rest of us. "Mark my words, that kid is going to wear the black belt someday. Every man in this room could learn from that kid."

Bill, the granite-faced man who had been my personal savior the night I came for my first lesson, raised his eyebrows and opened his eyes fully. It was the most dramatic change of expression I had ever seen from him. "That's your friend?" he asked me.

"Yeah," I said proudly.

"Yeah? Well, your friend has balls this fucking big," he said, stretching his arms out to their fullest extension.

At the end of that lesson, Sensei gave us all a speech about how difficult the road to mastery is, and how one must be prepared to give up everything if one truly desires to wear the black belt. He told us that he'd had to drive several times a week from Connecticut to Washington, D.C., to study with *his* master, sometimes driving all night to return in time for his day job. He had lost count of the number of bones he had broken over the years, and related for us the story of how his first teacher, an American, had committed suicide by first slicing open his belly with a samurai sword, crawling up a staircase with his intestines dragging behind him to the place where he kept his pistol and finally shooting himself in the head. "Death with fucking honor," Sensei commented at the end of this story, nodding thoughtfully.

Then O'Keefe gave us a rare treat; he said, "Listen up. When you people do the forms, you look like a bunch of old ladies, and then you wonder why you never use those moves when you fight! I'll tell you the reason. When you do these forms, you're supposed to do them like your life depended on it!" Then he showed us what he meant, executing a form so advanced and so secret that none of us even knew its name. He moved with lightning speed, and with each punch and kick the cloth of his uniform cracked like a whip. When he was finished, he stalked over to the heavy bag hanging from the ceiling and said, "The same thing goes when you hit the bag! Don't pat at it! If you want a nice mild workout, go take badminton lessons. This is kung fu, goddammit! When you hit the bag, hit it with everything you got!" By now he was really charged. He hit the bag about fifty times in ten seconds, each blow landing with a sound that made me nearly sick to my stomach. Then he let out a piercing scream, jumped up into the air, spun around and hit it with a reverse crescent kick that doubled the bag over on impact. For a finale he put an old towel on the floor, stacked up eight gray bricks over the towel, then splashed lighter fluid on the stack. He had Bill light the stack, then stepped back to glare at it for a moment. He started hissing from the pit of his lungs, sounding like a man being scalded alive. His feet were pulling so hard at the rug that it bunched up between his legs, and his face turned into a portrait of obscene determination. He hit those bricks with the edge of his hand so hard that he might well have just continued right on through the floor and severed the gas line. By the end of this demonstration I was convinced that no man on earth could survive a violent encounter with Timothy P. O'Keefe.

I thought I feared and admired this man more than anyone else in the world, but when I looked over at Michael I saw that I was wrong. My friend's jaw was slack, his eyes were bugging out of his head, and the ice pack he'd been holding to his elbow had fallen to the ground. Moses see-

ing the Burning Bush couldn't have looked more impressed. He was speechless all the way home, and when I
saw him in school the next day, he still could barely articulate words. "Let's work out this afternoon" was all he
said.

6

Although chagrined by having been overshadowed so quickly by Michael in Sensei's eyes, at the same time I was overjoyed to have finally found someone with whom to practice conventional male bonding. Quiet discussions over the telescope with my dad, stimulating though they were, simply could not substitute for affection disguised as aggressiveness, which every healthy boy craves. A useful analogy can be found among vegetarians who, wanting to break the cycle of violence wherever they can, feed their cats soy products, only to watch them lose their hair and become depressed. Cats are carnivores, like it or not, just as young men are weapons with legs. By the end of that week Michael and I were punching each other for hours every day.

We soon began sleeping over at each other's house so that we could start practicing kung fu the instant we woke up, resume practice after school, and keep at it until we couldn't keep our eyes open any longer at night. Our policy was that whenever we were both healthy we stayed over at my house, whereas if one of us had a black eye, a split lip or a sprained finger we stayed at his house. His mother, who had once been a gym teacher and was, after all, the mother of the Golden Horde, was used to seeing boys in various states of disrepair and patched us up without any fuss. My mother, on the other hand, would have had a fit if she knew how often I was jamming my fingers; what if I wanted to play the cello again once I'd gotten over "this kung fu thing"? She was tolerant of my bizarre interests, bless her heart, but she drew the line at bare feet in winter and bone fractures (of which I eventually had several).

Michael and I were perfectly matched for optimum competition between us. I was more graceful and flexible than he was, so I looked better doing the forms and individual techniques. Michael, on the other hand, always got the better of me during sparring because he was stronger and had superior fighting instincts, lots of previous experience and an alchemist's gift for turning frustration into pure aggression. Nearly every sparring session followed the same course: it would be an exciting, even exchange until the very end, when he would back me up against a wall with a furious onslaught of sloppy kicks and punches, finish me off by putting me in a headlock and boxing my ears, then cackle with delight and cry, "Once again the fine-boned Roman sentry discovers that his glittering armor, bronze weapons and volumes of Plato are no match for the fearless Hun and his rough-hewn spear! Better luck next time, Loserus Maximus!"

We tried to outdo, outlast or outsmart each other in every possible way, and endeavored to make our workouts as imaginative as possible. One of our "reflex" exercises was to go down to his basement, each put on one of his brother Larry's Mexican hats and ponchos (Larry's field of study was *los bandidos de la revolución*, and his bedroom walls were covered with black-light posters of Zapata, Guevara and Castro), light up a couple of cheap cigars and face each other like gunfighters. Michael had a portable record player down there, and for this exercise he always played the theme music from the Clint Eastwood movie *The Good, the Bad and the Ugly*. As the music built to a climax, we paced slowly toward each other. When we were only inches apart, we would blow smoke into each other's face as a rude challenge. We would throw down the cigars, toss the ponchos over one shoulder and wait, sneering at each other and squinting like Eastwood. When the tension became unbearable, one of us would finally say "Draw" and act—not by pulling out a pistol, but by trying to kick the other in the chest or face (the higher the kick the lower the chances of success, but the greater glory if you succeeded) before he kicked you. We came out about even in this exercise (we named it *The Loose, the Tight and the Chickenshit*) because although Michael was a bit slower, I was more nervous and started late about half the time.

One week Michael saw in the paper that a drive-in movie theater in Danbury was showing *The Twelve Tests of Shaolin*, a kung fu flick about the harsh training habits of the early Shaolin temple monks. We had to go, no question about it. We pooled our money but found we had enough for only one ticket, so we got his brother Frank, the former rocket scientist, to drive while we hid in the trunk. Once it got dark we crawled out, but unfortunately the pimply kid at the ticket booth saw us. He waited until the film started, then came over to our car and asked to see our tickets. When we couldn't produce them, he said, "I'm gonna have to tell the manager," and walked into the office connected to the refreshment stand.

Frank seemed unfazed by the situation; his eyes never left the screen. Michael suggested that we insist that we simply couldn't find our tickets, but I said the best thing to do would be to go straight to the manager and confess in order to avoid having him call the police—or worse, our parents.

"Are you *crazy?*" Michael asked, looking at me as if I were a complete idiot. I said I would go alone if I had to, but it had to be done as soon as possible because we'd been caught. When I got out of the car and walked toward the office, though, Michael followed me. "You're out of your mind," he kept saying.

We walked into the office and faced a fat, tired-looking man with a crew cut and a cigar in his mouth seated behind a large desk. I made our confession, explaining that we were poor kung fu students who were desperate to see the movie because we could learn from it. I said that we could prove we were really serious by giving him a demonstration in his office. He declined the offer, frowned at us menacingly, waved a plump hand in the direction of the door and said, "Go on, beat it. You did the wrong thing, boys, but I'm gonna give you a break this time. Go see the picture, but next time no clemency."

On our way back to the car, Michael looked at me as if I had just turned water into wine. When we sat down to see the rest of the movie, he shook my hand and said, "Man, all these years I've been getting caught doing stuff, and I never once thought of that! God*damn*, you're smart!" I left it at that, and from this point on Michael was convinced that my timorous personality was in fact a highly effective disguise. "You can get anything you want with that innocent act," he often said, and I always responded with nothing more than an ambiguous smile.

It turned out to be a great movie. The premise was that all monks ready for graduation from the temple had to pass through twelve rooms, each of which contained a challenge. One room featured a series of crossbows triggered by invisible wires strung across the floor of the room. Qualified monks dodged or deflected the arrows; monks who had slacked off in their training paid a heavy price. Other challenges included thrusting one's hands into a tub full of red-hot metal filings until one located the tiny pearl at the bottom, sparring while balancing on high poles over a patch of ground bristling with deadly spikes, and having to reach into a hole in the wall to grab a greased iron ball without having one's hand cut off at the wrist by a lightning-fast guillotine blade released as soon as the ball was removed from its pedestal.

Although we couldn't find any crossbows or guillotines in Michael's basement, we did manage to fill a hibachi grill with sand, put one of his mother's earrings at the bottom, fire it up and poke around in it with our hands for a while. All we got from that exercise was blisters. We also tried sparring while balancing on a two-by-four stretched across a couple of picnic benches; when that got boring we tried it blindfold, and wound up fighting with long staffs à la Robin Hood while balancing on a fallen tree stretched out over the lake. Another favorite game was sneaking out of our houses on nights when it was snowing, taking our sleeping bags out to the foundation of a burned-down barn and trying to sleep as the snow piled up on top of us. The first one to suggest going home was the loser. When we got back to his house, the loser had to serve the winner hot cocoa and give him a foot massage. It was all very Greco-Roman.

Eager to follow in the footsteps of the ancient masters, we speculated about how many of the martial arts schools had been founded by people who imitated the offensive and defensive movements of animals such as tigers, cranes, snakes, eagles and even insects. Michael's house was always filled with anywhere from two to seven cats, not counting kittens, so we began by studying them. I was appointed secretary of defense, which meant that it was my job to record their behavior in little notebooks with diagrams and verbal descriptions. Since most cat behavior is related to eating and sleeping, we found little to inspire us, but Michael noticed that if we provoked one of the kittens by dangling a piece of string in front of it to get it going, then dragged that string right over one of the sleeping adult cats, both kitten and adult would soon display the kinds of violent behavior we were looking for. As soon as we saw something interesting I would write it down; then we would rush out to the backyard and try it out on each other. We got pretty good at scratching each other, and Michael even experimented with a move where he wrestled me to the ground, held my shoulders with his hands and kicked my stomach with both of his feet.

One day, on a shortcut through a field while doing his paper route, Michael stumbled on a praying mantis, the inspiration for one of the most feared and respected kung fu schools of all. He rushed it home, telephoned me with instructions that I run to his house with my notebook, then began poking at it with a twig to test its parrying skills. When this strategy bore no fruit—the mantis didn't seem to mind being poked by the twig—we tried putting ants and beetles in front of it. Ours was either an unhealthy or a very well-fed mantis; it barely moved at all. "Maybe it needs to be in a fight," Michael suggested, so he took it out of the shoebox and put it on the nose of one of the kittens, hoping to start something. The kitten ignored it. When Michael put it on Rasputin's nose (Rasputin was an old tom with frayed ears, one eye and a forty-five-degree kink in his tail), the once-mighty cat looked at it cross-eyed for a second, batted it to the ground with his paw and swallowed it.

Ultimately, we never did learn any truly effective techniques from the wild, although Michael did have limited success for a while with a frenzied movement he called the Piranha Attack Sequence. As soon as I learned to counter it with the Net Across the Amazon defense, however, he dropped it from his arsenal and we stuck to what Sensei taught us.

The other result of seeing *The Twelve Tests of Shaolin* was that we decided to imitate the outlandishly complicated and spectacular fight scenes found in most Hong Kong kung fu movies. We always finished our serious practice sessions with one of these mock battles, to the point where we had a whole series of cues and responses worked out. One favorite sequence began with Michael's sweeping me to the ground, then trying to stomp on me, my grabbing his foot and tossing him backward, my getting up and trying to rush forward at him, but his jumping up at the last second, catching himself on the low branch of a tree, wrapping his legs around my neck as he hung there and then strangling me. The finale came when he let go of the branch and we crashed down together in a heap—always with me at the bottom, I noticed.

A few months after Michael joined the kung fu school,

Sensei O'Keefe announced that we were ready for our first belt tests. The ranking sequence at our school was white belt, yellow, blue, green, brown and finally black. Beyond that there were degrees of black; Sensei, for example, was a fifth-degree black belt.

Neither of us could sleep the night before our test, and we skipped school the next day to go over our techniques, our forms, and to practice breaking boards. Neither of us had any appetite for lunch or dinner. We had my mother drop us off at the Institute an hour early so we could warm up there; we spent most of that time out in the parking lot doing push-ups and egging each other on. Just before Sensei arrived, Michael pulled out of his pocket one of his treasured red bandannas and handed it to me. "Good luck," he said, and I felt my chest swell with pride as I put it on.

It seemed to go by so quickly that I barely remember the test itself. In retrospect it seems odd that we were so nervous, because we had trained so hard there was little question of our deserving our white belts. But Sensei O'Keefe was infamously strict about ranking, and regularly cursed the "shopping-mall karate schools" that handed out belts according to how many lessons you took or how much you paid. He would get so angry talking about those schools that I sometimes worried he would give himself an aneurysm.

Michael and I did our techniques, our forms, and broke several boards, then were told we would spar each other for the rest of the test. We hadn't expected this; we imagined we would be sparring with the other students going for *their* white belts, whom we knew we could make a good showing against. "This better be good," Sensei O'Keefe muttered, then took a seat next to two fearsome-looking black men, both of them wearing uniforms and black belts, who had been sitting there without making a sound during the whole test. They were Sensei's "special guests," men whom he had taught and awarded the black belt to years before. Now they were respected and feared teachers themselves, operating out of Norwalk and Bridgeport—cities well known for their tough neighborhoods.

Michael and I looked at each other and knew we had to come up with something. We started fighting, and as expected, Sensei O'Keefe started yelling at us for looking like pussies. Michael did it first; he gave me the signal that we used during our choreographed "kung fu movie" routines, and then attacked with a flying, spinning kick. I did my part, which was to roll underneath him and come up with a side kick to his upper back that sent him into the wall and then down to the ground. Noting the murmurs of approval from our audience, we proceeded. I jumped into the air as if to flatten Michael with my whole body, but he rolled to one side in the nick of time, did a somersault and put me in a headlock. I bit his leg, he let go, and then came the finale. I ran at him as if to choke him and he, taking me by the forearms, rolled backward and put his foot against my stomach so he could do one of those John Wayne flips that you see in cowboy movies. Our Hong Kong twist was that I used his arms as pole vaults and, instead of landing flat on my back, landed on my feet behind him. We turned to face Sensei and saw that he, along with his two friends, were holding their bellies and laughing so hard that no sound came out.

"They're the fucking bandanna brothers!" one man finally said.

"No, no, they're the fucking *judo-jitsi* brothers!" the

other guest insisted, recalling the term from one of the old *Bowery Boys* episodes. Now that we had been given a title, our reputation as an inseparable pair was sealed.

Becoming very serious all of a sudden, Sensei had us kneel in front of his guests and all of the senior students and asked in a booming voice, "Does any man here object to these students getting their white belts? If so, speak now, or forever hold your fucking peace."

"No!" they all shouted, and Bill the Giant gave us the thumbs-up sign behind Sensei's back.

"All right, then," Sensei said, and he had everyone kneel in one line. He put glasses in front of everyone and poured each of us a full double shot of tequila, gave everyone a slice of lemon and poured salt on his hand. He did the same for himself, making his more like a triple shot, however, then knelt in front of us and said, "May the Ancients smile on us, and speed us on our Path." He licked the salt, bit the lemon, then downed the glass, and we followed suit. It was my first taste of alcohol of any kind, and the instant I swallowed it I wondered why liquor had ever become popular.

We all spilled out into the parking lot, throwing kicks and doing push-ups and acting like five-year-olds. Within a few minutes the alcohol took effect, and then I knew the answer to my earlier question. Both high as kites, we wrestled in the backseat of my mother's car all the way home, then went on a barefoot midnight run around the lake to begin our weekend of celebration.

I had been helping Michael with his paper route for weeks, and together we had saved up enough money for a special treat: a Peking duck dinner for two at the Dragon Inn, the only Chinese restaurant left in Ridgefield after the

Rickshaw Inn out on Route 7 closed. We placed our order the morning after the white-belt test, and that night rode our bicycles, wearing our kung fu uniforms, new white belts and red bandannas, announced our arrival to a suspicious maître d' (how would you feel if two fifteen-year-old boys in kung fu suits and bandannas came into your restaurant and ordered a complete Peking duck dinner?) and had our feast.

We stuffed ourselves to capacity, then rode over to the ice-skating rink, where the annual Bavarian Beer Festival was being held in full force, complete with oompah band, old couples dancing the polka and beer served in huge pitchers by plump women dressed up as Bavarian hostesses. We managed to gain entrance by persuading a man in his fifties to say we were his kids. Once inside we were wondering how we could get one of those pitchers of beer, seeing as how we were obviously underage and had no money, when we heard someone call out our names. It was Larry and Don, Michael's number two and three brothers, and at least thirty of their friends. That's when we knew everything was going to be perfect.

For one glorious hour I was one of the Immortals, drinking beer, shouting, playing cards, swearing oaths of loyalty and staring in drunken amazement at every woman. After Michael and I had each finished a pitcher of beer or so (the *second* time that I had tasted alcohol) the two of us, with no dance partners and plenty of encouragement from his brothers, decided to reenact our judo-jitsi performance from the night before. It met with tremendous approval from our group, but got us thrown out of the Garden. We didn't care. We rode the five miles home on our bicycles, punching and kicking each other the whole way.

By the time we reached my house we were both feeling strangely dizzy, and wisely decided to press on to his house. A good thing we did, too, because we spent the whole night propped up against the bathtub with our heads drooped over the edge puking up beer, scallions, Chinese pancakes and pieces of duck skin. At exactly six o'clock the next morning Mrs. Dempsey marched into the bathroom and said, "Well, well, well. What a pretty sight. Since you're big enough to go out and drink too much just like big men do, you're big enough to get up on time and work like grown men have to. Michael, it's Sunday morning, the papers are already here, and people are waiting. I want you on your route in five minutes, and I don't want any mouth about it. Mark, it's not my business to tell you what to do, but I know you're not the sort of boy who'd stay all comfortable with his head in the toilet when his best friend is doing his paper route. There's coffee downstairs if you want it."

I never could have imagined that a paper route could seem so interminable. It took more than twice as long as usual; we had to walk slowly to keep our throbbing heads from moving up or down, took frequent breaks by the side of the road to catch our breath, and spent a good deal of time in the woods throwing up. When we finally got back to his house, we trudged up to his room, crawled into our sleeping bags and vowed that when we got our yellow belts, we would celebrate with clear soup, toast and ginger ale, and at all costs stay away from his brothers.

7

Drunk with confidence and ambition after receiving our white belts, Michael and I increased our efforts and made good progress over the next year. We practiced every morning before school, every afternoon after school, and even persuaded the gym coach to let us practice during school in one corner of the basketball court. We entered every karate tournament we could, subscribed to all the available martial arts magazines, saw every Bruce Lee movie at least six times, and on weekends helped Sensei O'Keefe give demonstrations in parks, church basements and at sporting events. He was losing money every month paying the rent for our building; the initial wave of interest in kung fu, set off by the Bruce Lee movies and the David Carradine television series, was already beginning to wear off, and the dropout rate at the Chinese Boxing Institute was high. When I first joined up there were nearly twenty-five students, but by the end of that year there were only three die-hard regulars—Bill, Michael and me—and about six who came sporadically. The demonstrations usually began with our doing forms, followed by our breaking up into pairs and sparring. Since these events were carried out for recruitment purposes, Michael and I refrained from using our more controversial judo-jitsi techniques such as leg-biting, hair-pulling and eye-poking. At last Sensei would call us into a line, bow to us, then to the crowd and deliver the goods. No one goes to martial arts demonstrations to see a bunch of students practice on each other.

Sensei usually started with a choreographed fight scene with either Bill or Michael or, at the larger events, one of his black belts from Norwalk or Bridgeport. He never used me in this part of the show because I was so tiny it would hardly have impressed anyone to see him neutralize me. Occasionally he would get a bit overexcited during these routines, especially if he'd had a drink or two or three before the show; once he jumped into the air, spun around and kicked Michael in the eye with the heel of his foot so hard it knocked Michael semiconscious and gave him the ugliest black eye I have ever seen. Assuming it was part of the act, the crowd rewarded Sensei and Michael with a standing ovation.

Next came the demonstration of control, which involved two of us getting on our hands and knees while a third, wearing no shirt, lay on his back on top of us with a watermelon on his stomach. Sensei would blindfold himself, do some loud breathing exercises, then split the watermelon with a samurai sword. It became an especially dramatic feat from our point of view if we could smell liquor on his breath as he did his breathing exercises.

After that Sensei ordered us to break a few bottles and

spread the jagged glass out onto a blanket. He stripped off the top part of his uniform and lay down on the broken glass, breathing even louder this time. Michael and I lowered four or five heavy concrete slabs onto his chest, then stood back as Bill rolled up his sleeves and lifted up a sledgehammer. Bill's Paul Bunyanesque arms flexed impressively as he took a few slow practice swings to build suspense. Then, after a final dramatic pause, he shattered the slabs on Sensei's chest with a mighty overhead stroke.

The climax was always the stack of flaming bricks. I never did get used to the sight of Sensei O'Keefe's face or the sound of his frenzied breathing when he prepared to break them with his hand. I used to imagine that a truly wild man, in the sense of having grown up without any social or cultural conditioning at all, would probably look and sound like that if he got cornered by a leopard in a cave. Every time Sensei did it my admiration for him, along with the suspicion that I could never be like him, swelled and left me feeling both satisfied and empty.

One night Sensei announced that he was going to run a weekend kung fu camp up in the mountains. Michael and I panicked when he mentioned the tuition cost, but managed to find enough neighbors who needed lawns mowed over the next two weeks so that we were able to scrape up the money just in time. Bill planned to go too, and was bringing a tent that would be big enough for all three of us.

Early in the morning on the day the camp was to begin, we all met in the parking lot of the Boxing Institute. It was just Sensei, Bill, Michael and me, but another group from Bridgeport was going to meet us at the campsite. Michael and I packed our sleeping bags, raincoats, swimsuits and extra clothes into Bill's blue van (it had a big decal in the back window of a guy wearing a beret and smoking a joint, the same zigzag design as the tattoo on Bill's arm), and Bill let us sort through his box of eight-track cassette tapes and put together a musical program for the ride up. Michael and I were arguing over whether we should start with Black Sabbath or Creedence Clearwater Revival when Sensei walked over and asked, "Any of you guys wanna ride with me?"

We were stunned. An invitation to ride for several hours with Sensei, in his sleek Mercury Cougar with the vanity license plate that read KUNGFU, was like a dream come true. There was so much we wanted to ask him but had never dared; by always seeming aloof and vaguely angry, he effectively discouraged most attempts at friendly conversation. One night during a lesson an "old buddy" of his burst into the Institute, jumped into a parody of a karate stance and with a huge grin on his face yelled, "Hey, Timmy! Look who's in town after all these years!" Without a moment's hesitation or so much as a word of warning Sensei jumped over the little wooden bridge, grabbed the man, sent him flying out the door and into the street and chased him until he was well out of sight. "Don't *any* of you fucking people ever make the mistake that man just did!" he fumed when he returned, his eyes black with rage.

So when Sensei asked if either Michael or I wanted to ride with him, Bill read the situation perfectly and said, "Hey, why don't both of you guys go in his car, because I have to make a couple of stops anyway to pick up food and lighter fluid and all that other crap. I'll meet you up there in a couple of hours." Once again Bill saved the day.

Michael and I were so excited that we could hardly speak as we climbed into the Cougar. Sensei put on his leather hat and aviator sunglasses, and roared out of the parking lot leaving twin streaks of rubber on the road practically all the way to the entrance ramp to the highway. He drove just the way we'd imagined he would.

After what we thought was a polite amount of time—we didn't want to seem desperate—Michael and I couldn't wait any longer and started asking Sensei questions. What was he like when he was our age, how did he first get interested in martial arts, and could he tell us any stories about his own master, a Hawaiian-born Chinese who had supposedly killed dozens of North Korean soldiers with his bare hands during the war? Michael and I saw this enormous man only once, at a martial arts convention where he stole the show by shattering a six-foot-high stack of ice blocks with his palm; to do so he had to stand on a folding chair, which got knocked out from under his feet when the huge chunks of broken ice came tumbling down.

Sensei answered most of our questions by saying either "Yeah" or "Nah" or by shrugging. After a few minutes of this he frowned and turned on the car radio, signaling the end of our interview. We spent the rest of the ride feeling terrible, convinced that we had blown our one opportunity to connect with the Master.

When we got to the camp Sensei set up his own tent and ate a lunch he'd packed for himself. Our food was in Bill's van. A few hours later the group from Bridgeport showed up and we started working out. More time passed, but Bill was nowhere to be seen. By nightfall Michael and I were getting worried, not to mention hungry and a bit cold. We had worn our uniforms on the ride up, including our flimsy cloth "Bruce Lee" shoes, which had gotten soaking wet as we exercised in the dew-covered fields.

At ten o'clock at night everyone got up from the camp-fire and went to their tents except for Michael and me. We hadn't had anything to eat since breakfast, and we were freezing. The only bright side to this that we could see was that Sensei would probably have to let us sleep in his large tent with him, giving us a chance to redeem ourselves somehow for our poor behavior on the ride up. Suddenly a pair of headlights appeared on the dirt road leading to our campsite. Michael and I practically leaped for joy, thinking it was Bill, but as the headlights got closer we saw that it was a compact car driven by a young woman.

It was one of Sensei's girlfriends. As soon as she got out of the car she and Sensei disappeared into his tent, and Michael and I knew we wouldn't be sleeping indoors. Then it started to rain. We thought about sleeping on the ground under Sensei's Cougar, but then saw that it was parked on a hill and that a small torrent had already formed between the wheels. We didn't even consider ask-ing the Bridgeport group if we could squeeze into their tent; they were inner-city black men—utterly mysterious and therefore frightening people to us—whom not even Michael dared look straight in the eye. When we sparred with them we always stared at their hands so that we wouldn't become paralyzed with fear. Out in front of their tent they had set up a little plastic bucket with a sign taped to it that said DONATIONS TO HELP "TINY" RAISE BAIL. Just as we began to despair, Sensei stuck his head out of the tent and threw us his car keys. We spent the night trying to sleep sitting up in the bucket seats, but the sound of the rain on the windshield was a constant re-minder that we were soaking wet and cold. At one point Michael said that if he could live his life over again, one thing he would definitely change was his decision three years earlier during our BB-gun war to keep that boy who had fallen through the ice a prisoner in the abandoned Chevy. "No wonder that poor bastard was so mad," he kept saying, his teeth chattering the whole time.

We agreed that the glow on the eastern horizon the next morning was the most welcome sight of our lives. The rain turned to drizzle, and at eight o'clock Sensei began our training. The exercise made our bodies feel warm except for our feet, which were kept frozen by our soggy cloth shoes. At noon, when everyone broke for lunch, Michael and I built a fire and made a rack over the flames with a few long sticks. We hung our shoes and socks from the rack, hoping that the heat would dry them out, and left them there momentarily when Sensei, taking pity on us at last, offered us some of his own lunch. Suddenly we heard gales of laughter from the Bridgeport group and ran back to our fire to see that our shoes, which had cheap plastic soles, had melted. They hung like long strands of chewing gum, with the cloth parts slowly burning. We had to spend the rest of that day and that night barefoot.

On the third and last day of the camp Bill finally showed up. When he saw Michael and me pale, hungry and shivering in our wet uniforms and wearing no shoes, he apologized profusely, but his disappearance hadn't been his fault. His transmission had given out on a lonely part of the highway and he didn't have enough cash with him to have it fixed by the local mechanic; nor did he have enough cash to pay for a tow truck to take him back to Danbury. He tried to hitchhike back, but got picked up by the police in some small town, and when they saw his tattoo they busted him and held him overnight.

Michael and I changed into dry clothes and spent the next hour eating everything in Bill's van. Then Sensei announced that the camp was over, and this time he did not offer to let us ride with him.

"Well, at least now we can listen to Black Sabbath," Michael said, trying to look at the bright side.

"No, we can't," Bill said as we climbed into his rental car. "This car doesn't have a tape deck."

8

I disliked the ninth grade nearly as much as I'd disliked the seventh and eighth grades, although being Michael's friend meant that at least I didn't get beaten up in the hallways anymore. Why did the subjects have to be so boring? Did adults do this on purpose? They made the world the way it was, and then made us learn the rules so we would make sure not to change anything! If I'd had to sit through a class five days a week called "Plucking All of Your Hairs Out and Arranging Them in Stacks of Prime Numbers," it wouldn't have seemed any better or worse than my actual classes. I still thought Lao-tse had the right idea when he said that if you stopped learning, your problems would be solved.

When I entered the tenth grade, however, I began to feel differently about academics. For this I must thank an enthusiastic but professionally doomed world history teacher who saw my interest in China and ran with it. His name was Richard Rowland, but the students knew him as Rick der Stick, a tribute both to his angular physique and the vaguely Germanic atmosphere of discipline that he insisted upon in his classroom.

At the end of our first day of class he called me aside for a moment. "I understand from Coach Anderson that you're *extremely* interested in China," he said. He had a severe crew cut, a prominent Adam's apple, a slightly frenzied look in his eyes and a habit of emphasizing key words with bold, choppy strokes of his right hand, which always held a piece of chalk between the index and middle fingers.

When I said that I was indeed interested in China, he asked, "Well, what are you *doing* about it, Mr. Salzman?"—chop.

I told him about the Boxing Institute, but he seemed unimpressed. "You can't grasp another culture just by learning an art form out of context like that. First of all, you've got to learn the language. You've *got* to learn Chinese if you're serious. I've heard that you *are* serious, but I want to hear it from you. How willing are you to *work*, Mr. Salzman?"

Now it was my turn to look frenzied. "You know Chinese?" I asked.

"I didn't say that, but that's not important. I want to know if you're willing to work this year, because if you're willing to work, and I do mean *work*"—chop—"then I might be willing to help you. But what I'm talking about would be in addition to the regular classwork in my class. I'm *not*"—chop—"talking about letting you substitute the curriculum."

"I understand."

"All right. Give me a few days to think about this.

There are a few people I want to talk to, and then we'll see what we can come up with. But let me emphasize that if I'm going to do this on my own time, I'll expect you *not to let me down"*—chop chop chop.

What Mr. Rowland came up with was this: first, he gave me the title of a book, *Speak Chinese,* published by the University of Beijing Press, and told me to buy it right away. He knew someone who had used this book and persuaded the man to lend him the set of flash cards and audiotapes that went with it. Mr. Rowland let me borrow the tapes, while he kept the flash cards. He suggested that we meet once a week after school in the teachers' lounge, where he tested my progress by flashing the cards with the Chinese characters on them at me and helped me wade through the chapters, supposedly written in English, explaining the rules of Chinese grammar.

Second, Mr. Rowland told me that he had just completed a summer graduate course in Chinese history at Trinity College to help get his master's degree. He had all the books and the syllabus for the course, and would be willing to lend me all of that, along with his classroom lecture notes, as long as I was willing to report to him weekly on my progress and write the two required papers for the course, one short and one long.

Third, and most exciting of all, Mr. Rowland told me about a clever and highly sophisticated game that had been invented by Dr. Robert Oxnam, the professor at Trinity he'd been studying with. Called the Ch'ing Game, it was a complex re-creation of the Ch'ing-dynasty government that required more than twenty players and took a week to play. Mr. Rowland had been using the game as the climax to his world history classes for several years, but always lamented that the student playing the emperor had never been sufficiently prepared to make the game truly dramatic. He promised me that if I completed the work for the graduate course he would let me be the emperor, guaranteeing that it would be the most memorable experience of my high school career.

Once I started learning how to speak Chinese I wanted to learn how to read it, and as soon as I began studying those characters I wanted to write them. I wrote them all over my notebooks during my other classes, all over my desk, and all over my pants. There was something deliciously addictive about trying to make them look just right—balanced and yet free, correct and yet unselfconscious, as if the strokes had fallen onto the paper instead of having been carefully drawn.

For the first time in my life I was reading real books, not textbooks prepared for adolescents. At first I was shocked by how much reading the course involved, and I was discouraged when I found out how difficult the books were to understand. Happily for me, Mr. Rowland did not allow me to stay depressed for long. Apparently he had decided that it was already a foregone conclusion that I would finish the course. "What, you think other people just pick up these books and read them without any trouble?" he asked me, waving his arms and rolling his eyes. "Everybody has to face this kind of complex thinking sooner or later—*everybody*!"—chop—"that is, if they plan to ever really *understand* anything. Of course it's hard work! That's what we're here for, hard work! Didn't I tell you that already? Sure I did, that's old news. What passages did you have trouble with?"

The difficulty was more than compensated for by the excitement I felt knowing that I was doing something any adult would have to respect, and the work soon became a kind of pleasure. One day Mr. Rowland said that he thought it was a shame that I wasn't getting academic credit for my Chinese-language study. He introduced me to a counselor, Ms. Rauson, who informed me that I was perfectly welcome to apply for independent-study credit. She offered to act as the administrative go-between if Mr. Rowland and I would put together a formal proposal, and once we had done so, she set up and led the committee meeting where I made my presentation, and eventually I was granted the credit. It happened that one of the teachers present at that meeting was my art teacher. He had noticed the Chinese characters and imitation Chinese landscape paintings scrawled all over my notebooks and pants, and now that he knew how serious I was about the subject, he had an idea of his own. He asked me the next day if, instead of doing the regular coursework in our art class, I would like to organize a course for myself to learn Chinese brush painting and calligraphy, the real kind done with brushes and ground ink instead of just a ballpoint pen.

When I told my father about this he was delighted; he welcomed any evidence that my interests might be shifting away from unarmed combat. One time he actually asked me if I would consider dancing instead of kung fu— "Look at Nureyev," he said hopefully, "now, there's a powerful guy."

Ballet. Man, you know the world is a confusing place when you're a boy and your dad tries to get you to switch from self-defense to ballet.

So Dad was excited about the Chinese painting. He helped me by taking out dozens of oversized books on Asian art from the library. Over several weekends he and I charted out "a course," starting with the basic brushstrokes and characters, then moving to traditional methods of painting trees, rocks, mountains, waterfalls and little Chinese fishermen standing on the prows of their sampans. The final exam of the course, we decided, would be to paint a whole scroll depicting a waterfall partially concealed by mist, with a rocky mountain in the background and a fisherman right in front, admiring the whole scene from his sampan. In one corner I would brush a few lines of calligraphy of my own composition—assuming my *Speak Chinese* book moved beyond vocabulary like "worker," "peasant," "Twelfth Party Congress" or "high-level cadre."

Before giving the art teacher my syllabus, I decided it would be a good idea to show him samples of the kind of work I would be doing. To do so I needed the proper materials, so one Saturday I got Michael to take the train down to New York City with me for an excursion to Chinatown. We ended up spending most of our time in a kung fu supply store admiring the swords, throwing knives and black-silk uniforms, but on realizing that we couldn't afford anything except one of the Jackie Chan posters, we moved on to a bookstore offering painting and calligraphy supplies. I got myself a brush, a stick of dried ink and a small grinding stone, and Michael bought a magazine called *Secrets of Internal Kung Fu,* which had on its cover a photograph of a bony old man with a wispy beard allowing himself to be run over by a minivan.

On our way back to the subway station Michael noticed a building that looked like a Buddhist or Taoist temple with its doors wide open. Peering inside, we saw three dozen or so old Chinese men sitting around a bunch of tables chatting quietly and playing chess.

"Hey, you're supposed to be learning Chinese," Michael said. "Why don't you try it out on those guys? Maybe one of them is a master. They might be talking about kung fu right now."

By then some of the men had noticed us and were giving us slightly annoyed looks. Deciding to give them a pleasant surprise, I marched forward into the room, stood at my full height and recited the sentence I knew best: *"Tongzhi! Nimen hao ma?"* which translates as "Comrades! How are you?"

To a man their faces turned beet-red with anger, and not one of them said a word in response. They simply pointed toward the door and waved their hands in disgust. Thinking I must have pronounced something wrong, I retreated in embarrassment and led Michael out of the building. "What did you say to those guys, you asshole?" he asked, obviously upset that I might have just offended a roomful of kung fu masters.

"I don't know!" I answered, but when I took a last look at the building before we rounded the corner I got my answer. High over the wooden doors hung a sign that said in English, OVERSEAS CHINESE KUOMINTANG ASSOCIATION MEETING.

"What does that mean?" Michael asked.

"Oh, man—Kuomintang is the name of the old government that used to rule China! Those are the guys that got chased over to Taiwan by Mao!"

"So?"

"So? I called them Comrades! That would be like . . . God, it would be like if some kid walked into our kung fu school and said to Sensei, 'Everybody knows karate can kick kung fu's ass.' Man, that was stupid."

"Some expert you are. Loser!"

Several days later, after filling a few sheets with some

shaky brushstroke exercises, I began to worry that the art teacher might still be unimpressed with my presentation and decide not to let me go through with the independent-study course. Realizing there were things only a trained Chinese painter could teach me, I took what I assumed was the logical step: I took my painting materials, rolled them up under my arm and rode my bicycle to the Dragon Inn, the restaurant where Michael and I had consumed our ill-fated Peking duck dinner earlier that year. I entered the restaurant to see the cooks and waiters seated around three round tables having a late-afternoon meal. Not wanting to repeat my earlier experience with speaking Chinese, I remained silent until one of the waiters got up and asked if I wanted to sit at a table or order something to go. I said that I wanted to ask his colleagues a question about Chinese painting.

He shrugged and asked for everyone's attention. With all of them staring at me I became nervous and forgot the carefully worded statement of purpose I'd composed on the ride over. Instead I said, "Um . . . is anybody here a Chinese-landscape painter?"

"Yes, I'm a Chinese-landscape painter."

A chubby, shy-looking young man stood up. He was wearing black plastic nerd-glasses and a clip-on bow tie that had settled into a diagonal position under his collar. His name was Tommy Wing and, I later learned, he was an art-department graduate of the Chinese University of Hong Kong. After college he had begun his artistic career by painting landscapes for a traditional Chinese greeting-card company, but when his parents, who lived in the States, fell ill he came here to work as a waiter for several years to help support them. When I showed him my exercises and asked if he could give me any pointers, he covered his mouth with his hand and started giggling uncontrollably. "I'm not laughing at you," he reassured me when he gained control of himself. "It's just that I think—you know—that this is kind of funny! I mean, I always thought that white kids were only interested in Chinese kung fu."

There was something terribly familiar about the tone of his voice when he said "kung fu." He sounded just like my dad. I decided to postpone telling Tommy about my other Asia-related interest until we got to know each other better. He fetched some brushes and ink from his car and gave me my first lesson right there in the restaurant.

Having gathered the proper materials and a university-accredited tutor, I made my presentation to the art teacher and was given permission to proceed with the project. These successes with the independent-study approach led me to wonder, Why not do this with every class? I tried to persuade my science teacher to let me practice acupuncture on myself instead of having to memorize the Krebs Cycle, but this proposal was met with less enthusiasm than my language and brush-painting projects. The metal-shop teacher would not let me build a broadsword, and when I asked my math teacher if I could skip class to work on the Zen puzzle "If everything returns to the One, to what does the One return to?" his only response was to ask, "What, are you on drugs or something?"

Word of my quest to transform high school into a kind of preparation for the Chinese imperial examinations gradually reached the main office. The vice principal called me in for a meeting and explained to me the strict federal and state regulations concerning the curriculum offered in each grade of every high school, regulations that he had no choice but to enforce. When I protested weakly (I was not the type to argue with a vice principal) by reiterating how enthusiastic I was about these unregulated subjects, and how much I was enjoying learning them as opposed to the state-approved courses, he sighed and looked tired.

He leaned back in his chair and said, "Try to think of the school as a huge ocean liner. It's out there in the ocean, it's overcrowded, the engine is overworked, but it's moving slowly in the right direction. Then imagine that one kid falls overboard. We simply can't turn the whole ocean liner around just for him. I'm sorry; you'll just have to stick with the regular courses."

Man overboard! I was going to have to drown in algebra, French and chemistry after all.

Adults tell you that school is not about learning particular facts, but about learning how to learn. When the time comes that a subject intrigues you deeply, they insist, you will be grateful for having developed the skills needed to master that subject. "Someday this will all make sense," they say. And they're right. The problem for all of us as teenagers, unfortunately, is that until we find that special subject we have to take their word for it, and that's a lot to ask when you're talking about memorizing the Louisiana Purchase, the atomic weight of uranium or the pluperfect-tense conjugation for verbs in other languages. How about the chemistry involved in photosynthesis? Yep—could be useful someday. Anyone read *Tess of the D'Urbervilles* lately? Now, *there's* an enjoyable book when you're fifteen, especially all the descriptions of the flowers. If a sailboat left San Francisco thirteen hours ago against a 5-knot current and a 4-knot breeze and is just now reaching Santa Barbara, 312 miles away, what was its average speed? Hey, couldn't you just ask the Coast Guard? That's their job, isn't it? It's a miracle any of us make it to the drinking age without having gone insane.

Even with my limited knowledge of physiology at that time, I knew that teenagers were designed for humping, fighting and little else, but the modern world asks that we put all that off until after high school. Instead we must fidget in uncomfortable wooden chairs and learn how to learn. As mentioned before, you're told it will pay off one day, but between the ages of thirteen and eighteen you cannot help wondering, What if it *doesn't* pay off? What if our parents, and their parents, were all wrong about what's really important? How will it ever end if no one questions it? And these are supposed to be the best years of your life.

9

W e're moving," Sensei O'Keefe said abruptly after class one night. He and Bill lit up a joint in the parking lot and sat quietly; Michael and I decided to take a few last whacks at the heavy bag for old times' sake. The rent had finally driven us out. Sensei had found another building, this one in Danbury on Main Street, which at that time was a depressed area. It was not an ideal space; the room was long, but only about ten feet wide, so the Circle of Fighting became the Sliver of Fighting. Better than nothing, Sensei said, so that weekend he, Bill, Michael, three other students and I moved the equipment to our new house. During the move I noticed that Sensei had thrown away several dozen old trophies, framed karate and judo diplomas and plaques. One wooden plaque, with his name engraved on it, caught my eye, so I pulled it out of the garbage and put it in my equipment bag to take home and put on my wall.

Sensei, who was seriously depressed and drunk quite a bit of the time that season, apparently saw me take the plaque out of the garbage can, but instead of being flattered he called everyone together and denounced me as a thief. "Barabbas, the Christian thief. That's your new name: Barabbas. Listen up, Barabbas. Don't you *ever* think you can do something without my knowing it." He poked his callused finger hard against my chest for emphasis. "I am the Master here, and you better get something straight. I can see right through you—I know what you think and what you do. *I know you better than you know yourself.*"

Instead of being mystified or impressed by something Sensei did, for the first time I felt annoyed. I didn't question his status as a kung fu master, I didn't object to his unusual training methods, like the time he had one man hang from the rafters with one hand and hold a paper target between his dangling legs with the other so that Sensei could practice archery, and I didn't mind his calling me a candy-ass or a sissy, but even I knew that he was no mind reader. As I put the plaque back in the garbage an unwelcome thought came to me: This guy can punch well, he can kick well and he can cut watermelons blindfolded, but what if underneath all that he's really just a jerk?

I did not express that thought to anyone, least of all to Michael. It seemed that the worse Sensei behaved—the more hostile and abusive he got—the stronger Michael's loyalty to the man became, as if he were trying single-handedly to make Sensei's life turn around by being the perfect disciple. On one of our first nights at the new school Sensei came in looking even more morose than usual. "I just drank seven fucking rusty nails," he said to no one in particular, then put on his uniform. Halfway through the class he announced, "I'm gonna show you guys how to defend against a fucking cartwheel. Mark, do a cartwheel at me." The cartwheel as an offensive maneuver is about the stupidest thing you can imagine; it makes you completely vulnerable to just about any counterattack, and besides, even if you do it successfully and hit the person with your ankles, it hurts you more than your opponent. I obeyed him, of course, and he defended himself by planting a hopping side kick into my thigh so hard that most of my leg turned black and I had trouble walking for over a week. That night I was so upset that I cried in the car on the way home (Michael had just turned sixteen, so we no longer had to rely on our parents for rides). "Don't be such a candy-ass," he scolded me. "You deserved it for trying to steal his plaque. That was a lesson to you, man—don't try to blame it on Sensei."

We lasted at that studio for only a few months before Sensei ran out of money and had to default on the lease. He told us that he had an acquaintance who could help us out; he never called anyone his friend. "I don't have any fucking friends," he liked to say with a combination of bitterness and pride in his voice, as if this were the unpleasant but inescapable burden all warriors "who don't give in to the bullshit" must bear. This acquaintance ran a bar near a lake, and said we could hold our lessons on the lawn behind the bar. In lieu of rent, Sensei worked as a bouncer after our classes. Learning kung fu on the grass behind a bar took away some of the romance from our lessons, and unrestrained access to rusty nails and tequila sunrises caused a noticeable decline in Sensei's skills.

One night Bill and I were sitting by the lake after a particularly bad lesson; either Sensei was in a foul mood or he just couldn't think of any new techniques to teach us that night. In any case, he had us spend most of the lesson doing punishment exercises like push-ups and crab-walking (where you crawl on all fours but with your chest facing upward rather than downward). To no one's great surprise, Bill crab-walked right over a broken bottle; there was glass all over the ground behind the bar. After the lesson, while pulling slivers of glass out of his palm, Bill sighed, looked back at the bar and said, "Pretty fucking seedy." Coming from Bill, who never complained about anything, this seemed a bad sign indeed.

"What's going to happen to us, Bill?" I asked.

He chuckled, but then fixed me with that stare of his that could stop a charging elephant. "We'll move on and we'll do just fine," he said evenly. "I've been with Sensei for six or seven years now. Having to watch him flush himself down the toilet is no fun, but it's his problem, not yours or mine. If he can't teach us, we'll find somebody who can. That's all there is to it. It's your buddy I'm worried about. Mike hasn't figured it out yet."

"Figured what out?"

"That Sensei makes his own fucking problems. You're smart; you figured it out, but I gotta tell you, Mark, your problem is that you let it show. That's why Sensei gives you such a hard time. But Mike still thinks the guy is God. It's because he doesn't have a father, man. You don't have to be Sylvester Q. Freud to figure that one out."

Once we made that final relocation, we stopped giving recruitment demonstrations for the Chinese Boxing Institute. We still went to tournaments, however, and Bill, Michael and I usually did well. Michael always came home with a fighting trophy, I with one for forms, and Bill either with trophies in both categories or in neither because he had been thrown out for "excessive contact." The way this always worked was that Bill would face the rare opponent who looked as powerful and tough as he was, and things would get rough. Neither man would protest, so the delighted judges would let it go the distance. Although he was usually smaller than the other man, Bill was always tougher, and in the end the judges would disqualify him for the inconvenience of having to revive the other man and wipe the blood off the floor.

We traveled up to Canada one weekend for a big tournament, and Sensei, Michael and I were invited to spend two nights in the apartment of a young kung fu teacher, one of the organizers of the tournament. He was a friendly guy who spent a whole afternoon teaching Michael and me some exotic combinations with names like Monkey Climbs the Tree and Splits the Coconut. This involved running straight at your opponent, stepping up onto his thighs as if climbing a ladder and then pounding straight down on his head with your clenched fist. The first night he stayed up until 4:00 A.M. with Michael and me, talking about kung fu and telling us about his own experiences as a student. Sensei was out carousing with some of his old buddies and didn't return until long after dawn. That day was the tournament, but Michael and I were so tired from having stayed up all night that we both bombed out early. The man we stayed with ended up winning the Grand Championship that night, though, with Michael and me at ringside shouting our lungs out and having a ball. Afterward a big group of us went to a restaurant to celebrate, then back to the champion's apartment. I thought it was to go to bed, but it turned out that Sensei just wanted to change before going out for some real partying.

"Hey, Mike, Barabbas, look alive. How would you

boys like to get your cherries popped?" he asked. "I met two nice ladies tonight who'd love to help a couple of kung fu students work on their internal energy!"

Michael and I both flushed red and declined. "Oh, don't be a couple of pussies! Come on, you wanna know what their names are? Auggie Doggie and Doggie Daddy! They both have false teeth, so they'll gum you if you're real nice!" He was having a great time, but our host could see how miserable Michael and I were, so he persuaded Sensei and the rest of his friends to let the two of us go to bed. "OK, but we're gonna bring Auggie Doggie and Doggie Daddy back here for you," Sensei promised. "If you feel something fat and warm and sticky crawl into your sleeping bags tonight, don't piss your pants!"

After they all left, Michael and I panicked. We were sure he was going to come back with those women to humiliate us, so we left the apartment with the idea of spending the night in Sensei's car, as we had at camp, but then we realized that this would be the first place he would look. We ended up finding a car with an open door at the far end of the apartment complex's parking lot and crashing there. Neither of us could sleep. At some point in the night Michael said, "If you tell any of my brothers about this I'll cut your balls off."

"Why would I tell them, for Chrissake? I chickened out too, you know."

"Fuck you! You chickened out, I didn't! I don't care, I could do that, no problem. It's just I'm not going to do it with somebody ugly."

"Yeah, me neither."

Silence for about ten minutes.

"OK, Barabbas, you're the smart guy. What the fuck does it mean?"

"What?"

"That they're gonna 'pop our cherries.' What the fuck is the cherry?"

"I have no idea! Why do you think I'm sitting down here? It's probably some weird thing where they stick something like a cherry up your ass and then pull it out and eat it. I don't know."

Michael's face puckered and creased up so violently that he looked like a shih tzu dog. "Fuck that! I am *never, ever* gonna watch somebody eat something that came out of my ass!"

"Me neither," I hastened to agree.

"Jesus! There'd be *shit* all over it! What the fuck's the matter with those people? Man, now look what you did— you made me want to puke! What'd you have to tell me that for, you asshole?"

"You asked, so I told you! It's just a guess, I don't know."

Silence for another ten minutes. Then Michael, looking out at the empty lot and shaking his head, muttered, "I hope that's not part of the black-belt test."

The school year passed quickly; I made it to the end of *Speak Chinese*, Volume I, finished the readings and wrote the papers for the Chinese history course, and completed not one but several scrolls featuring T'ang dynasty poets standing on mountaintops admiring mist-shrouded water-falls. In fact, I took to paying for my kung fu lessons by selling the paintings for twenty or thirty dollars apiece. I found customers by hanging them from the branches of trees at local Arts and Crafts fairs, sitting underneath them and playing the cello to attract attention. My best customer of all, ironically enough, was the vice principal of the high school. He couldn't turn that ocean liner around for me, but he wasn't going to let me starve out there on the water either. He bought paintings every time I showed up at one of those fairs.

What I was really waiting for was the Ch'ing Game, scheduled for the next-to-last week of school. No one in our world history class had any idea that I had been doing all of that preparatory work, so I looked forward to surprising everyone by making the game especially fun by being a damn realistic emperor. I knew how the ministries of finance, war, agriculture and foreign affairs operated, and I had carefully planned out what to do in case of internal rebellion, barbarian attack, famine, flood, locust infestation, or even my own early demise due to sickness or assassination. The game required that for the entire week we twenty-five students would be excused from most of our other classes and had to stay in character all day long while Mr. Rowland, who played The Will of Heaven, challenged us with the unexpected. The most attractive aspect of the exercise was that for the first time I (who had never been chosen with any enthusiasm for even so much as a softball team) would be in a position of social status, and I planned to make good use of the opportunity. I wasn't going to be an asshole emperor, a corrupt, paranoid, harebrained despot like so many of the real ones; I intended to be such a wise, humane, competent and good-humored emperor that it would be remembered long after the game was over, particularly at prom time.

My only worry was that during our weekly after-school sessions I had noticed a change coming over Mr. Rowland. He seemed preoccupied, as if he had found something more interesting than world history but couldn't decide whether to tell me about it or not. A month before the Ch'ing Game he confided in me: he had become a Christian Scientist and was experiencing supernatural visions. While reading the newspaper one morning the word "Lebanon" suddenly leaped right off the page and hung in the air in front of him, he told me, then seemed to explode and bathe him in a shower of dazzling light. Another day he leaned forward and asked, "You saw that it was raining out today, didn't you?"

"Yes."

"When I rode my bicycle to school this morning, the rain parted for me."

"Wow."

"It can't be a coincidence. I'm thinking of giving up all of my material possessions and going to Lebanon to help."

All I could think was You've been so good to me, if you want to give everything away and wander the desert in rags I won't say a word to anyone, but just hang on until the Ch'ing Game is over.

Two weeks before the game was to begin Mr. Rowland led a student government club field trip down to Washington, D.C., for the weekend. On the morning they were to leave he got frustrated by how slowly the hotel was checking the group out, so he called in a bomb threat from his hotel room, thinking that this would be one way to get everybody into the charter bus quickly. It was a disaster—he was fired immediately, and our substitute teacher, who had never heard of the Ch'ing Game, finished out the year with a series of lectures on the Soviet Union. Several weeks after the hotel incident Mr. Rowland showed up at my house one Saturday morning looking gaunt but determined. He had several huge boxes tied to the back of his bicycle.

"I'm leaving for Lebanon tomorrow. These are all my books about China from the M.A. courses I took," he said. "I won't be needing them, obviously, and I think you ought to have them." Most of them were university press hardcovers; if bought new, the collection would have cost thousands of dollars.

"I don't know how to thank you," I said.

"Well, do you have any money? Those were pretty expensive books."

"No, actually. I don't have any money."

He grinned. "That's OK! Just thought I'd ask. Hey, sorry about the Ch'ing Game. You really worked hard for that. But that effort wasn't wasted, I guarantee you. You'll know what I mean someday. I guess not everything works out the way you want it to, though, huh?"

There it was again: my father's philosophy, leaking out even in fanatical Christianity. Rick der Stick got on his bicycle, waved good-bye vigorously, then rode off to the wars, and the summer officially began.

10

The summer of 1975 was especially hot and humid, making my daytime workouts with Michael and our evening lessons at the lakeside bar almost unbearable. We worked out a system of reward and punishment where, if one of us scored a point on the other, he got to dip his bandanna in a pail of fresh cold water or run underneath one of the neighbors' lawn sprinklers, while the loser had to do push-ups in the sun. Immediately after lessons we ran straight into the muddy lake and stayed there for half an hour. When we climbed out of the water, one of Sensei's friends who worked at the bar always had a bottle of Blue Nun sitting in an ice bucket waiting for us.

After Bill's comment about my attitude toward Sensei showing through too clearly, I made an effort to be respectful of the Master and more understanding of his situation. It was true that without realizing it I had developed the idea that I could pay my tuition and learn all of his skills without having to pay attention to him as a man. But in his own inarticulate way Sensei was letting me know that I couldn't learn his skills if I didn't accept the whole package. If I ever wanted to fight like him, or break as many bricks as he could, I was going to have to think more like him and appreciate what had brought him where he was.

That summer I tried to look at him in a different light, to convince myself that even though his behavior and thinking were different from mine or my father's, they were still legitimate in their own way. My father was often depressed, and I respected that, so who was I to say that Sensei's morose hostility was bad?

I think Sensei noticed my attempt to change my attitude, because that summer he did start to treat me better. He began speaking to me without using sarcasm in his voice or acting as if he were talking to a baby, for example, and when he explained techniques he would look me straight in the eye without glowering. My sparring ability did improve slowly, and once I began winning matches in tournaments he took to standing by the ringside with his arms folded and watching, nodding when he approved of something I had done and coaching me with hand and eye signals.

Just as I was beginning to feel more comfortable around Sensei, however, an accident occurred that threw me right back into a state of moral confusion. A brown belt who was formally studying karate with someone else but who had known Sensei for many years was in town one night and joined us for a workout. It happened that one of Sensei's black belts from Norwalk showed up on the same night, and the two of them decided to work on their sparring after class. They were both competitive, and with Sensei watching closely there was a lot at stake. In sparring somebody often gets a little over-excited, or moves forward at the same moment that the other throws a punch, so that he gets hit a little harder than he would have liked. Then the pace steps up. This is what happened that night. After a few minutes we heard another hard hit and the pace went up another notch.

"Everything cool here?" Sensei asked.

"Yeah, fine," they both said through gritted teeth, so Sensei let them continue.

They slowed down a bit, but not for long. About three minutes after the pause the pace built up again. The black belt spun around with a spinning back-heel kick that was meant to whiz past the other man's face, but the brown belt unexpectedly darted forward at that exact moment. The kick landed right on his mouth with a sickening crunch. He fell backward, and when he sat up we could see that the lower part of his face was caved in. Blood and teeth were everywhere.

Showing no sign of panic, Sensei picked up all of the teeth, made sure that the man could be safely moved, then calmly led him to his Cougar and raced him to the hospital. Eventually he had to have both his upper and lower jaw rebuilt, his mouth wired shut, and most of his teeth replanted. We were told he wouldn't be able to eat solid food for a year. For several weeks thereafter I had a difficult time sparring because I was so afraid of being hit in the face, and some nights I could barely make myself go to lessons. Even Michael seemed shaken for a while.

The summer ended at last and I started the eleventh grade. Without Mr. Rowland championing me I had lost some academic momentum, but two new teachers quickly picked up where he had left off. One was Al Leighton, a no-nonsense U.S. history teacher with a booming voice and loads of charisma who thought it was about time that I focused some attention on my own culture, and the other was Jacob Friedman, a language teacher who had been on sabbatical the previous year. During our first day of French class he explained that he had spent his sabbatical year in Taiwan, realizing a long-standing dream of learning to speak, read and write Chinese. It took an effort of will for me to sit still for the rest of the hour; when the bell rang I practically knocked him over when I rushed to his desk to beg him to help me with my Chinese. He agreed, as long as I didn't mind having our lessons out in the corridors during his hall-monitor duty, a task he was only too happy to augment with learning.

Just before Christmas I turned sixteen and got my driver's license. The day after my test I asked a girl on a date and she said yes. Her name was Annette Guillaume, and I had first met her on one of my fruitless missions to her older sister Marie's house. I'd had a crush on Marie for years—she was in Rick der Stick's class with me—but she was permanently attached to an older guy who owned his own Volkswagen bug and had driven it to Mexico and back. One winter afternoon I rode my bicycle over to Marie's house to say hello just in case anything had changed with the older guy (who was all of eighteen), but no, there he was in the living room talking with Marie's mother about socialism. It was blizzarding out and I was covered with snow, so Marie said I should borrow some of her brother Jean-Rodolphe's clothes and change down in the basement. When I went down there I scared her younger sister, who was also changing into dry clothes after spending the afternoon sledding. I saw only her face, but that was enough. A month later, when I got my license, I called her up and asked if she liked Chinese food. I figured she'd be impressed when I told her that our waiter was also my painting teacher.

Our date was a success, though in an entirely unexpected way. I suppose I had fantasized that my first real date with a girl where we were alone in a restaurant and then in a car would be—or at least should be—worth writing about and sending off to *Playboy*, but instead what happened was that we started talking, and kept talking, and simply couldn't stop talking, and I enjoyed every minute of it. Annette was smart and funny and, to my surprise, a lot like me: she got interested in things easily but was bored with school, she wasn't very popular because she was seen as a goody-goody, she played a classical instrument and she liked her parents. To my adolescent male confusion, I realized that she seemed less interested in my kung fu skills than in my study of brush painting and calligraphy.

When I drove Annette home she invited me in. I knew from experience that you didn't just pop in to the Guillaumes' house in the evening; you had to be prepared to think and talk intelligently. An evening there was like hanging out in a Paris café around the turn of the century. Annette's father was a French Moroccan Jewish doctor—he'd patched me up after several of my kung fu mishaps—who smoked a pipe, played the violin and always had a recording of Bach's violin sonatas and partitas playing in the background. Her mother was a German Catholic doctor (my sister's pediatrician) and gourmet cook who wrote fiction in her spare time. Their three children were functionally trilingual, and they always had interesting people in their house sipping espresso, eating one of Mrs. Guillaume's homemade tarts and discussing either art or international politics. I hesitated to enter; with my extremely long hair, double-knit Sears bell-bottom pants, dirty sneakers and swollen knuckles I worried that, having just taken their daughter out on a date in my dad's rusted VW bus, I might fare poorly at Café Guillaume. As soon as I stepped in the door, however, Annette's father nodded with approval, made a skyward flourish with his pipe and mentioned how much he had enjoyed my mother's last recital. How glad I was that she played the harpsichord and not the accordion, and how glad I was that I finally had a girlfriend.

Michael made no attempt to conceal the fact that he thought that Annette was pure trouble. Trouble in the sense that I would have to spend time with her when I should be working out. He was sulky for a few weeks and gave me the cold shoulder for the first half hour of each time we met, but once we got practicing, everything was like the way it had been before. In the meantime his brother Frank had decided to join us on the Path of Kung Fu. He was a student at Fairfield University by then, majoring in medieval studies, and managed to find us an empty classroom with mats on the floor that we could use for lessons. Sensei checked out the place and gave it the nod; we would all miss the Blue Nun parties by the lake, but it was getting too cold to work out in the open anyway.

Frank also managed to find two complete suits of armor built for kendo, Japanese bamboo-sword fencing. The heavy suits were made of metal, bamboo and canvas and protected you from head to toe. Sensei was delighted; these suits would allow us to practice all-out, no-holds-barred fighting without the danger of accidents like the one that had crushed Brown Belt's face earlier in the year. I hated fighting with those suits on, however; they were hot and cumbersome, and hard to see out of. Often you would get kicked in the head full force without even knowing a foot was coming your way, so you couldn't even tense up to receive the blow. Most of all, I dreaded sparring with Bill when we wore those suits because even with sixteen-ounce boxing gloves on his hands and twenty pounds of armor on my body, a punch from him was an experience that I had no choice but to savor for days afterward.

Having a roof over our heads improved Sensei's mood for a few months. One night after class he handed Michael and me certificates for our green belts without testing us at all. "I'm not giving you these because you deserve 'em," he said. "I'm giving 'em to you to see what you'll do to earn 'em." As he walked away he added, "But I wouldn't give 'em if I didn't think you would earn 'em."

His improved mood did not last long, however, and soon he was back in his funk, wondering aloud why he wasted his time with pussies like us and telling us over and over that not a single one of us would have lasted five minutes in the schools at which he had learned. "I give you two guys green belts and what happens? You slack off! You know what I had to do for my fucking belt tests? A couple of senior students would drive me to a fucking bar out in the middle of nowhere, pick the biggest motherfucker in there, go over to him and say, pointing at me, 'See the guy over there? He just said you're a fucking scumbag piece of shit,' and then they'd sit back and watch. I let you guys off so fucking easy, and what do you do? Jerk off all day, that's what. Why I waste my fucking time I'll never know."

I must confess that in a sense Michael was right: Annette *was* trouble. Having an intelligent girlfriend made what I was going through at the Chinese Boxing Institute seem a whole lot less attractive. She never said a thing about it; it was just her presence—self-assured, relaxed and together in spite of not having the least idea how to break someone's neck—that made me wonder how I had gone from wanting to be at one with the universe to letting a borderline sociopath scream at me twice a week.

The decisive incident was Sensei's lesson in strangulation. "I never taught any of you guys how to cut off somebody's windpipe," he said one evening after our warm-up drills. "I want a volunteer. Who'll let me knock him out?"

I didn't think he could be serious, and even Michael looked uncertain. There was an awkward silence as we all grinned nervously, which only enraged Sensei.

"I said I wanted a fucking volunteer!" he roared. "What, is *everybody* in this place a fucking pussy? I've been knocked out so many times I can't even count—and by God, if I ever hesitated when my teacher asked for a volunteer he would have beaten me so bad I would have been in a hospital for a fucking week! So I'm gonna ask one last time, *Who's gonna fucking volunteer?"*

"I will, Sensei!" Michael blurted out. He jumped forward and stood at rigid attention to make up for his earlier indecision.

"Sit down in front of me," Sensei said curtly.

Michael obeyed and Sensei came up from behind him, wrapped his arms around Michael's neck and squeezed. Michael struggled to keep his arms at his sides, but as his face began to lose color he lost control and started to claw at Sensei's arms. The Master was wrapped around him like a python, however, and could not be budged. In reality only a few seconds passed, but it seemed to take forever for Michael to lose consciousness. His eyes bugged out of his head and his body twitched and writhed in panic, but at last he went still, his eyes wide open and glassy. It was a shocking sight. I looked over at Frank, who was staring quietly at his unconscious brother with his arms folded tightly in front of him. Bill was frowning; this time he was the one letting his attitude show.

"This is how you revive a guy," Sensei said. He reached around and slapped Michael hard in the diaphragm, and like magic my friend popped straight up into the air. He was a bit disoriented; "What's everybody looking at?" he asked several times. He didn't remember any of it, and seemed to think that Sensei had not yet carried out the demonstration. Everyone was a little uncomfortable after this. It might have been my imagination, but I thought that even Sensei appeared a bit subdued for the rest of that night.

That turned out to be my last lesson. I was upset over the strangulation tutorial, because it was obvious that we hadn't *learned* anything. Who didn't know that if you strangle a guy he'll lose consciousness? And the slapping-the-stomach part—well, he could have just *told* us that and we would have believed him, for God's sake. It was such a stupid way for Sensei to vent his temper that I knew I couldn't continue with the lessons. I spent the next few days drafting a letter to him thanking him for what he had taught me and apologizing for letting him down, but explaining that the Path of the Warrior just wasn't for me. I walked over to Michael's house as I always did before we drove to lessons and handed him the envelope and asked him to give it to Sensei.

"What is it?" he asked benignly. He had no idea what I had been brooding about.

"I'm quitting lessons."

At first Michael thought I was joking. When he realized that I was serious, I saw where the expression "his face fell" came from. It was as if all the muscles in his face went loose, and he looked about five years old.

"You're cradding *lessons*?" he asked, in a strange, thin voice. "Cradder" was a word he had made up to describe the sort of person who takes karate for a few months, practices on weekends and then quits when it gets tough. Here he had turned the word into a verb.

"Yeah, I guess I am." I held my breath waiting to see what his second reaction was going to be, and when it came it was pretty much what I would have predicted. His expression turned to one of sheer disgust.

"Sure, I'll give him the letter, cradder." He put it in his pocket, climbed into his car, slammed the door and drove away, leaving me to wonder how to spend my first Thursday night in nearly three years away from him.

11

Once I had cradded lessons, and without Michael to practice with or compete against, my commitment to martial arts began to weaken. Neither Annette nor my family, nor her family nor anyone else, for that matter, seemed disappointed that I was no longer training to become an ass-kicking motherfucker. That made me wonder if the whole thing hadn't been a mistake to begin with. I told my dad one evening as we tried to find the planet Neptune that I had doubts I would ever become a black belt.

"You mean you're not going to be able to break flaming concrete slabs after all? I was counting on that, you know."

"It's not funny! I just wasted three years for nothing."

"What do you mean? You had a good time with that kung fu stuff, didn't you? You can't expect everything you try to lead to a finish line somewhere. You have to take a few wrong turns, hit a few dead ends, get mad and turn around. Everybody does—we're all the same that way."

"Oh, yeah? What about you? You liked astronomy and painting as a kid, and here we are looking for a planet through the telescope and you paint every night. You don't seem to have hit any dead ends."

"Hold on, I think I see something. You want to go get the nine-millimeter eyepiece?"

Got him. He was stalling for time to think. I went to the car to fetch the eyepiece, but this time, instead of walking the way a cat walks, free and easy, I was shuffling. It was an all-too-familiar teenage situation: I was arguing a point with my dad and felt driven to try to win the argument, but if I did, it meant that I was right about something depressing—in this case that three years of my life had been a sham.

He put the eyepiece in and looked for a while. "Here, see if you can see anything."

I looked, but couldn't tell if the dim object in view was a planet or just a star made to appear slightly fuzzy by our unstable atmosphere.

"I think if it was Neptune, we'd know it, Dad."

"Yeah. If we had just a few more inches of mirror. . . . Oh, well." He backed up and looked upward, presumably deciding what to look for next.

"So you think I haven't hit any dead ends, eh?" he asked abruptly.

"I never saw any pictures of you wearing baldhead wigs or trying to eat peas with sticks."

"Well, OK. You have more . . . panache than I ever did, I'll grant you that. And yes, I was lucky to find two things that I've stayed interested in all my life. But what about this: I chose social work as a career because I thought I could save people or solve their problems. I had big ideas; I was full of compassion. By the time I realized how hopeless the situation is—or at least how hopeless I think it is—and saw that it was a dead end, I'd driven so far down the road I couldn't afford to back out. So be glad you wore your wig and ate peas with sticks early and didn't make kung fu your college major. Now you know you won't have to do it for a living."

"Dad, you're talking about college. What were you like when you were my age? Come to think of it, I don't know anything about you before I was born! You've never told me anything about what you were like as a kid. I don't know any stories about your childhood at all."

He kept looking for Neptune.

"Well?"

"Well what? There's nothing to tell."

"That's no answer."

"Yeah, it is. I was moody and shy and not very interesting. Just like now. What else do you want me to say?"

At first I tried to keep in shape on my own, but instead of being a challenge, as in the old days, kung fu had become tedious. Every punch and kick felt sloppy and slow, as if I had weights strapped to my limbs, and I felt winded all the time. It was a dead end. Once the kung fu practice stopped, everything else followed. I stopped brush painting (all of a sudden I wondered, Why the hell am I painting little guys with robes and topknots staring at waterfalls? I've never even seen a waterfall, let alone a guy with a topknot), put the Chinese history and philosophy books into the crawl space and suddenly found it ludicrous to think that while even Stone Age tribesmen wore moccasins, I was going barefoot. I kept up with the Chinese lessons, but only because I liked Mr. Friedman so much and felt guilty about having already let one teacher down.

Every once in a while I would see Michael in the hall, the cafeteria or outdoors. I would nod at him or try to start up a conversation, but he wouldn't acknowledge me: I had ceased to exist. Sometimes I could see him stretching or practicing kung fu out on the football field, and I wanted to join him, but it was clearly impossible. As far as I knew, he didn't have any other friends; whenever I saw him, he was always alone. I often thought about calling him up, but then I could hear the litany of abuse he would heap on me, how I was a loser, a cradder, a candy-ass and so on, and decided I'd had enough of that crap.

As the fall turned to winter, I started to feel blue and tired and yet strangely anxious all the time. For the first time in several years I didn't know what to do with myself, didn't feel interested in anything, hated getting up in the morning, hated going to bed at night and watched lots of television. Dad understood perfectly; when he saw me stretched out on the couch he would pull out the Green Blanket, whip up some cinnamon toast and Constant Comment tea with milk and sugar and join me to watch old movies. My mother was less sympathetic. She'd been willing to let me burn incense in the basement, she'd driven me for years to kung fu and cello lessons, she'd even helped me powder my baldhead wig—but she could not stand seeing me mope. She hated it when I complained that there was nothing to do because there was so much to do! So much to read, so much to learn, so many instruments to play, so many rooms to clean! Whenever I passed her in the house—I on my way to make more toast or find *TV Guide*, she on her way to make oboe reeds for her students, tune her harpsichord, wash our whole family's laundry or start dinner—I felt myself slouch a bit, like a dog tucking its tail between its legs after having destroyed a sofa. The more I slouched, the straighter she stood, until the two of us looked like cartoon characters named Good Girl and Bad Boy.

My only relief came on the afternoons when I visited Annette and we took walks together in the kind of idyllic fall scenery that you see on postcards advertising New England. When we returned to her house, there was always something homemade to eat waiting for us on the table, and someone with unusual ideas or an unusual accent to talk to. She and her parents all seemed to think that I should return to the cello, which I hadn't played much during my enrollment at the Boxing Institute. Dr. Guillaume in particular seemed eager for me to give music another try. He played with an amateur chamber orchestra that could always use another string player; besides, he pointed out, with my cello, his violin and Annette's flute we could form a trio.

I decided it couldn't hurt to try, so I pulled the cello out from under the piano one weekend, blew the dust off it and tried to play some Bach. Awful! This wasn't the answer. I put it back under the piano and turned on the television. Intending to watch *The Six Million Dollar Man*, I inadvertently stumbled on a program in which the violinist Yehudi Menuhin was playing a concert with the Indian musician Ravi Shankar, who sat on the ground playing a sitar. Something about the unusual music appealed to me, so I kept it on and then listened with interest to the brief explanation of how ragas worked. To me the extraordinary thing was that though each raga, or song, had a fixed basic melody, every time they played it they improvised on it and played it differently. I don't think I had ever heard real improvisation before. My experience had been that all music was played from notes written down by some Immortal hundreds of years ago who was unappreciated in his time and died in poverty.

At the end of the program I went back down to the basement and took out the cello again, but this time sat on the floor and laid it across my lap like a sitar and tried to improvise. With my typical flair for immediate fixation, I didn't emerge from the basement until late that night, having decided to become an Indian musician.

My mother was overjoyed when I told her that I was serious about the cello again, but less enthusiastic when I showed her *how* I was playing the instrument. "Better that than shooting drugs, I suppose," Dad thought aloud, and she had to agree with that. Erich's only comment was "Leave it to Mark. Out of the frying pan, into the fire." Only Rachel approved of my new hobby. By then she was disappearing into her bedroom for weeks at a time to paint watercolors and listen to Beatles records, so she no longer found me strange at all.

Once again Dad helped out by scouring libraries, only this time not for kung fu manuals or brush-painting textbooks but for records of classical Indian music. In the meantime I took the cello over to the Guillaumes' place to show them my new interest.

"*Eh? Non!*" Dr. Guillaume protested, waving his pipe in front of him as if to ward off danger.

"*Ach, ja!*" Mrs. Guillaume countered, grinning from ear to ear. The weirder I got, the more she seemed to like me. But Annette liked it best of all. She went out to a fabric store the next day, bought a few yards of Indian-print cloth and a pattern called "Nehrudelic" and sewed me a shirt that made me look like Siddhartha before he gave up the comfortable life.

Gradually my depression vanished, but with the memory of existential angst still fresh in my mind, and the fact that I was improvising every day, it was inevitable that I would soon discover jazz. When I did I was even more excited than when I'd heard Ravi Shankar's performance. Before long I was listening and playing along to recordings of Chick Corea, Weather Report, Jan Hammer, Stanley Clarke, Jaco Pastorius and the Mahavishnu Orchestra. I set up the record player in the living room and tried giving my parents a demonstration, but their reaction was subdued. My mother looked at my dad and said, "That's really pretty interesting, I guess, isn't it, Joe?" My dad hesitated for a moment. Then he raised that eyebrow of his and asked me, "Has anyone invented an electric cello yet?"

"No, I don't think so."

He nodded, obviously relieved. "Then yes, I'd say it's interesting for now."

My new problem became money. I needed records—lots of them—to play along to, and the ones from the library were invariably scratched or warped. Also, as I spent more time with Annette, I could see it was getting on my parents' nerves that I was always having to ask for cash for gas. Even worse was when my dad would trudge out to the car in the morning, start it up to go to work, then see the needle below E and the TANK EMPTY light glaring at him. On more than one occasion I peered out the basement window nervously and could see his face in the predawn darkness, illuminated by the orange glow of the TANK EMPTY light, and by lip-reading I was able to appreciate just how much he did control himself when he was aggravated but not by himself in the car.

I scoured the papers for job listings, but couldn't find anything for an unskilled sixteen-year-old. I tried driving around the nearby towns and asking storeowners if they needed a hand, but nothing panned out. Finally one man said, "Try in Danbury. That's almost a city, so you might find something there."

I spent days driving around Danbury, passing by all of the former sites of the Chinese Boxing Institute. All of those spaces were still vacant, just as we had left them years before. One even had our heavy bag still hanging from the ceiling. Danbury was a depressed area indeed. At last, in an alley, I found the entrance to a hole-in-the-wall vegetarian restaurant called the Royal Embassy of Ooh-Aah. It was run by followers of the popular guru Sri Chinmoy, so there were pictures of him all over the place with offerings of plastic flowers, and fruit and incense burning in front of each loving portrait. The Royal Embassy staff took me on as a dishwasher, then trained me to wait on the five or six tables, and before long had me cooking, too. They were nice enough people, but they insisted on my joining them for their Sunday-morning staff meeting, which involved hand-holding, humming and lots of positive reinforcement. That was the worst part of the job, as far as I was concerned, and I didn't even get paid for it.

Obsessed with music now, I began to spend less and less time on schoolwork, and Mr. Leighton, the charismatic history teacher with the big voice, got worried.

"Mr. Salzman," he boomed after asking me to join him in the faculty lounge, "I get the sense that you are losing interest in your studies. What's the deal?"

I told him about jazz and he rolled his eyes melo-dramatically and shook his head in mock dismay. "You're doing *what*? No wonder you're always wearing that kooky shirt. Give me a break, Mr. Salzman, that's a very nice hobby, I'm sure"—he rolled his eyes again— "but holy Toledo, pal, don't ruin your shot at getting a good education now, when it counts! You're a junior in high school this year, and your grades are important. You can play jazz all you want next year when you're a senior. Hell, everybody else will be either necking in the back-seats of their cars or killing brain cells with beer anyway, so why shouldn't you play jazz *cello*? Just put it off for one year, that's all I ask. What can I say to you to get you back to work?"

I promised him I would try not to forget academics al-together, but the more I thought about it, the more I real-ized I didn't want to waste any more time in school. I'd been the man overboard long enough! I'd already put in eleven and a half years learning things that didn't mean anything to me. I wanted to live my own life, I wanted to play jazz all day, I wanted to cut my own swath through life, blaze my own trail, use my own conscience as a com-pass—like Daniel Boone, or Bruce Lee, for that matter. All of my heroes took risks in order to follow their own muse; I had to get moving before it was too late and I got sucked into the rat race.

"Dad, I'm sixteen now and pretty serious about music, and you know, I've been sort of playing the cello since I was seven, so it's not like this is all *that* sudden or impul-sive—in fact, in a way you could say that my whole life led to this. So I've been thinking that maybe I should do music full-time now. What do you think about my dropping out of school just for a few years to give it a try? I could always go back and finish if it didn't work out."

Dad sighed, pushed his coffee cup to one side, folded his hands in front of him at the kitchen table and looked at me with all the self-control and weighty reasonableness he could muster. Still, I did notice a tiny, throbbing vein in his forehead where I hadn't seen one before. "Mark," he said in an eerily calm voice, "I have only seventeen years to go before I can retire. I'd love to survive that long, even just to get up that first Monday morning and realize, I can go back to sleep! Don't give me a heart attack, OK? Just let me live until then. What do you say?"

That was the end of that. There had to be a way, though, and as I passed the guidance office on my way to French class one morning I got an idea: What if I could get accepted by a college a year early, making my senior year unnecessary? Instead of actually going to the college, I could postpone matriculation indefinitely while I made my stab at a musical career. If I made it, I wouldn't ever have to actually go to school again, but if my musical career didn't work out, I would still have an education waiting for me and that vein on my dad's face would stay down in the meantime.

I stepped into the office and asked one of the counselors if I could have a few college applications. I was thinking primarily of the University of Arizona in Tucson, because my dad's oldest brother lived out there and I had always liked him, his wife and the desert.

"It's kind of early for applications," she said, "I don't have many of the forms in yet. How about MIT? No? Georgia Tech? No? Let's see—liberal arts, I have one here for Yale. They send theirs way early."

Why not? I took it home and spent a weekend filling it out, but the more I worked on it, the more unrealistic it seemed. I sent it off on Monday morning, asked Mr. Leighton and Mr. Friedman to write recommendations for me, and promptly dismissed the idea as harebrained. A month later the counselor stopped me in the hall and informed me that more application forms had come in, but I had decided by then not to bother filling out any more.

A month or so later I got a call from Yale asking when I could come in for an interview with an admissions officer, a standard part of the application process. Feeling like someone who had carried a prank too far, I chose a date and, when it came, drove with my father on a rainy Saturday morning to New Haven. We stopped first at the Yale Art Gallery to see *The Night Café,* a disturbing painting by Van Gogh that Dad had always loved. After admiring this and other gloomy paintings for a while, we returned to our car to find a soggy parking ticket tucked under the windshield wiper. "But there's still two hours left on the meter!" my dad yelled.

"Yeah, but it's a two-hour meter, and we've been here an hour and a half already. It must be broken."

"What! But that's bullshit, how are we supposed to know that? They can't . . . ! Goddamn those . . . Oh, let's get out of here."

Everything was going pretty much the way I'd expected it to.

We found the admissions building and Dad offered to wait in the car. "I don't want to get another ticket in this shithole city," he fumed. He hated cities.

I walked in and gave my name at the reception desk. A young woman who seemed not much older than me stuck her head out of a door and invited me to join her in a tiny room decorated with a poster from an exhibit of Chinese antiquities. When she asked if I would like some coffee I realized she was the secretary for the professor who would interview me. When she returned with the coffee, we chatted and it turned out that she had been a Chinese-studies major. She was enthusiastic about Chinese art, and before long we were really getting into it. I couldn't help wondering, though, when the fun was going to end and I was going to have to leave this delightful secretary and move on to a dark, wood-paneled room to face a glum, rheumatic professor wearing a robe and a black mortarboard hat who would ask me, "So, young man, why don't you tell us what you think a person—such as *yourself*—could do for Yale?"

After half an hour the young woman looked at her watch and said, "Oops! I have an eleven-thirty who's probably in the hall waiting. Well, I don't mind saying that I enjoyed our interview a lot. I think you'd love this place. Good luck!" And that was it—that was my interview.

When I went out to the car, Dad was still angry about the ticket, and I could see he was preparing himself for the bad news that my interview had been a disaster.

"How did it go?" he asked stoically.

I didn't know quite how to describe it. I just started giggling.

"Well?"

"I think it went pretty well," I said.

"Mm. That's good. Well, they'd better accept you," he said, pointing to the ticket on the dashboard, "or I'm gonna come back here and stick this up some dean's ass."

12

Over the winter I saved two hundred and fifty dollars from the restaurant job and decided it was about time I had my own car. I knew nothing about automobiles except that I wanted something sleeker than our VW bus, so when I saw an ad in the paper for a 1969 Triumph Spitfire for two hundred dollars, I went right over to the fellow's apartment complex, took what I thought was a careful look at the car and handed him my money. After I'd paid for it and signed the papers he advised me not to drive it very far because it burned oil *real* fast, but hastened to remind me that the Michelin tires on it alone were worth the two hundred dollars, and anyway it shouldn't take much to get it running again, probably just a gasket somewhere. I drove the thing home in a cloud of black smoke and called up Lenny, a guy I'd met through Michael who knew everything about cars.

Lenny, who had dropped out of school the year before

and worked at both a gas station and an auto-parts shop, came over and after about five minutes said, "You'd better take this car back. It needs a whole new engine." I tried calling the guy who'd sold it to me but he didn't answer the phone. "So what do I do?" I asked Lenny.

"Well, you could try to rebuild it. I rebuilt an engine once; it's not so bad. It's a small engine—we could pull it out ourselves if you want." He fetched some tools out of his car and we undid the bolts that held the engine to the frame. We disconnected the clutch, pulled the engine out and, since my parents didn't have a garage and it was already winter, carried it into the basement next to the harpsichord. After we set it down on a sheet of newspaper, Lenny had to get to his shift at the gas station.

I went upstairs and checked our tool cabinet to see what we had. Three regular screwdrivers, one Phillips head screwdriver, two pairs of needlenose pliers, an adjustable wrench, a ruler, a wad of rubber bands, a dried-up tube of Super Glue and some old sandpaper. My dad wasn't the handy type. It would have to do.

I went out to the car and pulled out the owner's manual, which had an exploded-view diagram of the engine. I figured that I would take the engine apart, see if anything looked drastically wrong, replace any obviously worn parts, then put it back together again. I decided to remove the oil pan first. I undid the bolts and pulled off the pan, then watched in numb horror as five quarts of filthy oil gushed out onto my sheet of newspaper, covered it instantly and spread out all over the basement carpet. Fortunately my mother had put little cups under each leg of her harpsichord in case the basement flooded during heavy rains, so at least the oil didn't ruin the instrument.

An inauspicious beginning, to be sure. I dismantled the

engine completely but saw nothing wrong with it. In fact, the parts looked great to me; I had no idea how precise the fittings were. Hoping that maybe just putting it together again would cure whatever its problem was, I set to work with my flimsy tools. According to the manual, several of the major bolts were supposed to be tightened to exact pressures with something called a "torque wrench." Not having one of those, I just tried to guess. When the manual said, "Tighten head bolts to 35 psi," I found something in the basement that weighed about thirty-five pounds (I checked by using our bathroom scale), held it in my hand for a while and then tried to approximate that pressure when I turned the adjustable wrench. Several gaskets were supposed to be replaced, but I figured with all that pressure the old ones would hold just fine.

When it was done I called Lenny up and we put the engine back in. When I told Lenny how I had "rebuilt" the engine, he didn't make any comment, but just grinned. When the time came for me to start the engine, though, I noticed that he stood well back from the car.

"What, did I do something wrong?" I asked, beginning to worry.

He shrugged innocently, but didn't step any closer.

I turned the key in the ignition, and—it started. It sounded beautiful! I revved it up a few times and glanced at Lenny, looking forward to the expression of astonishment on his face. Instead I saw an even bigger grin where the astonishment should have been. I looked behind me and saw, through the yellowed and cracked plastic convertible-top window, a cloud of black-and-blue smoke that threatened to block out the sun for our whole neighborhood. Apparently, I hadn't fixed the oil-leak problem.

When Lenny told me what was really involved in rebuilding an engine, I calculated that it would take five hundred dollars in parts, a thousand dollars in tools and about two years' worth of auto-shop courses before I could actually drive the car. Before he left that day, Lenny helped me push it into the weeds at the end of our driveway. "If you're not going to be using them or anything," he asked, "could I have those tires?"

The fifty bucks I hadn't wasted on the Triumph I spent on jazz records, and through Lenny I met someone who played the synthesizer and who had been looking for a bass player for some time. His name was Scott and, besides jazz, he was pretty seriously involved in Zen, Taoism, cabalistic theosophy, Carlos Castaneda and something called Magick, which involved warlocks, incantations and elves. We got together, improvised for a few hours and decided to meet a couple of times a week to practice. After each session we ended up talking about philosophy and religion, and before long the subject of drugs came up. I confessed that I'd never even smoked pot, and to my surprise he thought that was cool—I'd been into "a purity thing" with the kung fu, he observed, and purity was definitely powerful—but now that I'd been through that, he thought I might consider trying pot, but not as entertainment. He said it was amazing how it helped meditation, and how it made philosophical texts that had previously made no sense at all suddenly as transparent as spring water. Pot didn't have to be just something to do on a Saturday night; it could be a powerful psychological tool.

I was interested but hesitant. Frankly, I was afraid. My dad had told me that when he was in the air force he saw a guy smoke a joint and lose his mind, and the thought of losing mine and then having to explain to my dad that it was because I had done exactly what that foolish soldier had done was too awful to even think about. I told all of this to Scott, and he said, "That's cool. But listen, if you ever change your mind, do me a favor, will you? Don't decide to give it a try when you're at a party and some-body passes you a joint. That would spoil it for you; it would be so lowlife that I guarantee you'd be disap-pointed. If you want to try it sometime, call me up and we'll go out to one of the lakes and do it right. If you're out in a relaxing place with somebody who's into the kind of thinking you're into, you'll be fine. After all, you don't have to be high to freak out in the army—I'd freak out stone-cold sober if I had to march around all day with a crew cut and call people 'sir,' wouldn't you?" He had a point.

Scott and I got along well, and before long we were playing several times a week. He introduced me to an-other friend, a talented jazz guitarist who had already been accepted at the Berklee College of Music in Boston, and the three of us got a few songs into working shape, but we couldn't perform because I didn't have an ampli-fier for my cello. For the time being, however, we were satisfied to play quietly in Scott's room, then make tea and talk late into the night. Besides, I wasn't ready to make my move with jazz yet—I needed time to develop a wider repertoire of licks. So it was just as well that I didn't have an amp because I might have been tempted to rush into a gig, only to be disappointed with the results.

The Miracle occurred on a Wednesday afternoon late in the spring. On my way home from school I opened the mailbox and there was a letter in it from Yale. I took a deep breath, opened it and learned that I had been accepted for the class of 1980. I wandered into the house in a daze. My mother was teaching a piano lesson. I stood in the living room staring at her while her student, a plump little boy who always carried a briefcase, groped his way through a Chopin waltz. My mother noticed me staring and gave me a disapproving glance, but nothing reached me in my fog. At last the waltz ended. "What is it, Mark? I'm teaching, you know."

I held up the letter. "You won't believe this! Remember that application I filled out a few months ago? Well, it worked! I just got into Yale!"

Now it was her turn to look as if she'd been knocked on the head. "Whaaat?"

When I told her the news again, her jaw dropped and she covered her mouth with her hand, dumbfounded. "Better call your father," she finally said.

I had never had occasion to call Dad at work before. I reached a secretary at the school where he worked and she said she would page him. After a few minutes he got on the line and I could tell he thought it was the highway patrol calling to say that I, along with my mother and brother and sister, had been wiped out in an accident.

"I'm fine, Dad. You won't believe this, but I got into Yale."

"Whaaat?"

So I told *him* again. There was a long pause. "OK, let's not get excited yet. Would you do me a favor? Call the admissions office and check. They might have stapled your application to somebody else's or something. Make sure about it, Mark. Then call me right back."

I called the admissions office, and they assured me that my application had not been stapled or glued to anyone else's. When I called Dad back and told him, he was speechless. When I pressed him for a quote, he said, "Well, some dean in New Haven is breathing a little easier now, because I held on to a copy of that parking ticket just in case. I really was going to stuff it up somebody's ass if you didn't get in."

Everybody was in a good mood that night, but only I knew that we were celebrating for different reasons. My parents were happy because they could go to sleep knowing I was going to attend an Ivy League college, whereas I was glad because I would be finished with school forever in about four weeks. Soon, if I liked, I could realistically attain my earlier goal of forgetting, rather than learning, something every day. I had no intention of going to Yale; I saw the acceptance letter as a means of distracting my parents long enough to get my jazz career going. Once I was making good money, they'd be fine. The only problem was how I was going to explain to them that I wouldn't be going to New Haven in the fall. I decided to hold off on that for a while until I had a watertight strategy and a damn good speech worked out.

I spent those last few weeks of high school struggling to keep the grin off my face. It was the least I could do for my classmates, who had another long year to go. Michael's mother, who still worked in the cafeteria, heard the news through the faculty grapevine, and one day, as I bought a Popsicle from her, she said, "Michael's over there. Why don't you tell him the good news? He'll be so proud of you."

I didn't see how Michael would enjoy hearing about it—we hadn't spoken in almost a year—but I couldn't avoid the encounter now that his mother had suggested it. I went over, sat down next to him and said, "Can I tell you something?"

"What?" It was just what I had expected; he didn't even look up from the magazine he was reading.

"I, uh . . . I got into Yale." Boy, did I not think this was a good idea.

"Great."

That was it. I waved at Michael's mother so she would know I'd done it, she waved back, and then I left the cafeteria.

When the last day finally came, it was, as most long-awaited events are, anticlimactic. I handed in a history paper, picked up a few final exams, cleaned out my locker and said good-bye to my favorite teachers. When I visited Mr. Leighton in the faculty lounge, he leaned back in his chair, closed his eyes and put his palm against his forehead in the manner of a fortune-teller. He opened one eye and said, "This, by the way, is a strictly unofficial prediction. *Strictly* unofficial, do you understand? We never had this conversation." Then he closed his eyes and started to sway back and forth like Johnny Carson doing his swami routine. "What do I see? What do I see?" he murmured, but his voice was so resonant that even sotto voce it echoed down the hallways.

"Aha!" he yelled, lurching forward. "I see brain cells! Many brain cells! And look—no, how can it be? Yes, it is! They're dying! Many brain cells, dying over the long, hot summer! Now I'm pulling back out of the brain and I see . . . Mr. Salzman, and he is . . . enjoying himself in the company of other happy teens! Disgusting! I can't stand it any longer. . . ." Then he frowned, as if concentrating harder. "Ah, now I see farther ahead—he is studying in the library at a prestigious university. It is late at night; he is applying himself again, as we all know he should. All is well. Excellent, excellent." He pretended to shake himself out of his trance. "Good luck, Mr. Salzman," he said, shaking my hand so vigorously that I could feel it in my ankles, "and remember, that was a *strictly* unofficial prediction. I don't want any calls from concerned parents, if you know what I mean." Then he winked (it was 1976, before winking became uncool).

Right around this time all the matriculation forms for college started arriving, including the financial papers. My parents had to submit copies of several years of income-tax reports, and that's when my father began to realize that he somehow had to come up with the money to pay for the Miracle. A letter came announcing that the financial-aid office had awarded me an extremely generous scholarship, but even so, and even with the money I had saved from the restaurant (minus the amount wasted on the Triumph), I knew we didn't have enough to cover the rest.

One evening just before dark I was sitting out in the dead body of the Triumph remembering what it felt like to drive it that one time when Dad came out to join me. He looked terrible; I could tell right away he was feeling guilty about something. I could almost see his hair turning from jet-black to white in front of me.

"Mark, I don't know how to tell you this . . ." he began. It was awful for him.

In a flash I saw the opportunity in its gloriously unselfish disguise. "Dad," I interrupted, "I think I know what you're going to say, but before you do I want to tell you something. I've been thinking. Maybe it would be a good idea for me to postpone going for a year and work in the meantime to save up the money for school. The reason I think that would be a good idea is that I'm only sixteen years old, and all of the other freshmen are going to be seventeen or eighteen. I've already had to suffer through public school being the youngest and shortest kid in the class, so why should I make college the same? I mean, there's no huge hurry, is there? Even if I postpone a year, I'll still be a year ahead of everybody else. Then I can spend more time playing the cello and seeing how it goes. What do you think?"

He sighed. "Have you really been thinking this, or are you just saying it to make me feel better? I really feel like I've let you down."

"I swear," I said, and it was the truth and nothing but the truth but just not quite the whole truth, "that I've been thinking about postponing from the day this whole thing started. I didn't mention it because I was afraid you and Mom would hit the ceiling."

"Well, I'd rather you went right away because I think you'll love college and I don't think the age thing would be a problem for you—that matters less and less as you get older. But things being the way they are, I guess that's how we'll have to do it. I'm sure glad you're not disappointed, though."

"To be honest, Dad, I couldn't be happier."

With that out of the way, at last I could do what I wanted all day long. What I wanted turned out to be waking up at almost noon, playing along to records in the afternoon and then either going out with Annette or practicing with Scott at night. Within a month I was bored and restless beyond my wildest dreams. I needed something more, something that challenged me intellectually and spiritually, something exciting that would . . . lead me through the doors of perception to a brave new world, perhaps?

Everybody except Annette and Michael was stoned all the time that summer. In fact, sometimes it seemed that everybody had been stoned since the ninth grade except me. I was the only guy in my industrial-arts class who wasn't making a water pipe out of plumbing fixtures; I was always trying to make incense burners or kung fu throwing stars. I listened to the right music, I'd read the right books (in junior high I took Abbie Hoffman's advice and stole his book titled *Steal This Book*), I was the right generation (I'd watched Woodstock live on television when I was nine, only to be ridiculed by Erich, who danced around me for years afterward singing, *"Mark wants to be a hippie, for that's the way he was born!"*).

Clearly, I had been avoiding my destiny all those years. As Scott had said, purity was a phase I had gone through, but like all phases it had to give way to exploration and growth. Sooner or later destiny must be faced squarely. One night at a garage party, with the stereo blasting Aerosmith and somebody's drunk mother dancing like Salome while two guys pointed flashlights at her boobs, someone passed me a joint. I couldn't even count the number of joints I'd held; I was even quite good at rolling them. I'd spent many parties seated in a strange kitchen under fake Tiffany lamps rolling joints for everybody else—I just never smoked them. This time I brought the crooked white stick to my lips and nearly puffed at it, but then I remembered what Scott had said: If you change your mind, don't smoke a joint at a party. It would be too lowlife—call me first. I looked at the party and saw that the mother was peeling off her blouse while her husband, who was too drunk to stand up and stop her, cursed helplessly from a La-Z-Boy chair held together with duct tape. Yes, I could imagine reacting like my dad's air force buddy under these circumstances. *Call me first.* I passed the joint along and asked to use the host's phone.

13

Scott closed his eyes for a moment and appeared to be concentrating on something just before lighting his carved wooden pipe.

"What's that for?" I asked. My heart was beating wildly. I was afraid that I might have a bad high, and also nervous that we might be caught. The latter scenario was unlikely, however. We were sitting in front of a little campfire we had lit on the beach of the lake, only a few yards from where I used to practice with Michael. No cars could reach there, and it was a quiet, moonlit night—we would easily have heard or seen anyone coming.

"I'm asking the spirit of the lake to show us a good time," Scott answered, grinning. "Every time I smoke, I consider it a lesson. I learn things when I'm stoned, and nature is the teacher. If you're good to nature and pay attention to it, it will be good to you and show you amazing things."

He lit the pipe and inhaled deeply, then handed it to me. The moment of truth. Was I really going to do it? All those drug films we'd had to watch in elementary school were playing out in my head like a videotape on fast-forward. A puff of marijuana and the next thing you know, *bam!* you're popping pills, shooting heroin, snorting coke and then selling it. Then *clang!* that's the sound of the jail-cell door closing behind you, and after five years you get out and realize that your life's over, it's finished, you'll never be the way you were, so you go back to the drugs and die from an overdose in a slimy alley in New York City. What if those films were right? They made it sound as if that was what would happen to you if you smoked a joint, but no kid is stupid enough to believe that this happens to everybody, or even to the majority. It's probably more like one in a thousand. But what if I'm the one out of a thousand? There's no way of knowing beforehand. What if I freak out tonight and jump in front of a car because I think I'm Superman? Somebody had done this, I'd heard. I imagined my parents getting the call, I pictured their stricken faces. It was horrible.

Then I inhaled. I have no idea how the decision was made. One minute I was forcing myself to watch an imaginary movie about my own self-destruction, and the next I was puffing on that pipe for all I was worth. Just one more unexplained mystery of the human mind, I guess.

I never finished taking in that first lungful because halfway there I coughed so hard and so suddenly that I blew the whole bowl of pot out of the pipe and into the lake. I had a coughing fit that lasted half a minute, and I realized that it was *just like the first scene of all the drug movies.*

That didn't stop me from trying again as soon as I

could. I took a tiny puff this time, and managed to hold some of it in before giving in to the irresistible coughing.

After four or five shallow puffs I waited, but nothing happened. Scott had his eyes closed and was smiling. "Has it hit you yet?" he asked.

"No. I don't feel anything."

"It's coming, it's coming, don't worry."

Five minutes passed, then ten, then fifteen, then half an hour. I was extremely disappointed. Having gone through the exhausting exercise of visualizing my arraignment on drug charges, followed by my grisly death in the South Bronx, I wanted my drug experience, by God!

"Anything yet?" Scott asked, still grinning. He'd been grinning for the whole half hour. Didn't his face get tired?

"Nothing." After forty-five minutes I'd had enough of sitting there watching Scott grin. I decided to tell him that it was getting late and I wanted to head back. To make it realistic I made the gesture of looking at my watch. With my mouth opening to speak I suddenly stopped dead; my watch said 9:35 P.M. We had arrived at the spot at 9:30. It wasn't possible.

I put the watch up to my ear, but it was still ticking. Scott started laughing.

"And so the lesson begins," he observed. "Let's do the Time Warp!"

His laughter did not reach me in the form of sound, but seemed to pour out of his throat like a warm, thick liquid that ran all over my body. The fire lit his face from below, and where his eyes and mouth should have been there were fathomless black holes. Instead of feeling afraid, I was overjoyed. It worked! The world was completely, utterly different from what it had been before. Come to think of it, I too was completely, utterly different from what I had been before. I felt like a ghost; I could sense my body, and was aware of my thoughts, but instead of the usual situation of feeling that "I" was those thoughts inside the head of that body, "I" was something invisible and with no will or intentions at all, in a separate dimension from even my own thoughts, hearing my thoughts as if they were coming out of a speaker in the center of my head.

"Look at the trees," Scott said. I looked up and saw that the trees were arranged around us in a *perfect* sphere, a flawless bubble of leaves, with us at the absolute center. It was too perfect to be real, and yet it *was* real; I knew I wasn't hallucinating because each of the separate leaves, branches and trunks looked normal. And I knew Scott hadn't led me on purpose to this spot, because *I* had led *him* there. I had no idea what to make of it.

"How the hell did this happen?" I asked, honestly shocked. I'd read the Castaneda books too, but everybody knew they were just good fiction. What was going on?

"Nature is teaching us," he said, looking around. "I think the lesson is that everything is a circle, and all points in a circle lead back to themselves, so everything is connected to everything else. What do you think?"

MY GOD! I thought, THIS IS INCREDIBLE! THIS IS ABSOLUTELY INCREDIBLE! EVERYTHING IS IN-TERCONNECTED: THAT WAS THE MESSAGE OF TAOISM AND ZEN, THAT WAS THE MESSAGE OF RELATIVITY THEORY, THAT WAS THE MESSAGE OF QUANTUM PHYSICS. OH, MY GOD! THE TREES ARE SHOWING ME THAT IT'S TRUE!

All that Asian mysticism I'd read and tried to convince myself that I was understanding—no wonder I was always so disappointed! I didn't understand anything! THIS was understanding, and it was a TOTALLY different kind of understanding from anything I'd ever felt before. Every philosophical concept I'd ever been interested in, instead of being an abstract theory that one had to slowly build up confidence in, had been instantaneously transformed into a physical, visible, audible, tangible concrete fact. No, it wasn't philosophy, and no, it wasn't enlightenment—it was reality! It was THIS! Enlightenment was only a name, only a word, only an intellectual idea I'd developed. This was REALITY, and now that I was perceiving it this way, it was obvious why people who'd had this vision couldn't describe it or communicate it through words. Words were not the same as experience, and . . . OF COURSE! THAT'S WHY *THE TAO THAT CAN BE TOLD IS NOT THE ETERNAL TAO!* Because no verbal description of this could ever make someone *feel* this way!

"What's your lesson?" Scott asked.

"OH, MY GOD! YOU'RE RIGHT! THIS IS A LESSON! OF COURSE YOU'RE RIGHT! WHY WOULD I HAVE EVER THOUGHT THAT THE WAY TO LEARN ABOUT REALITY WAS FROM BOOKS OR FROM OTHER PEOPLE? IF YOU WANT TO LEARN ABOUT REALITY YOU HAVE TO LEARN FROM REALITY! OH, MY GOD, SCOTT, THIS IS THE MOST UNBELIEVABLE MOMENT OF MY WHOLE LIFE! MY WHOLE LIFE WAS WORTH LIVING FOR THIS! I'M HERE AT LAST! OH, THANK YOU, THANK YOU, THANK YOU!"

Scott laughed. "Don't thank me, man. Thank your teacher. Let's go look at the water." It was midsummer and the water temperature was perfect. The night air had cooled down so that the water was exactly the same temperature. We pulled off our clothes and dived in, and I felt as if I had just jumped into a cosmic wormhole leading me through a black hole into an entirely different universe. As I swam I immediately started imagining what it must be like to be a fish. Then I realized, I AM A FISH! WE'RE ALL FISH! WE THINK THAT BECAUSE WE'VE EVOLVED INTO MAMMALS AND THEN HUMANS THAT WE'RE DIFFERENT, BUT WE'RE STILL RELATED JUST LIKE I'M RELATED TO MY BROTHER!

I felt convinced that I was not merely imagining what it felt like to be a fish, but was actually having a genetically encoded memory of what I really had felt like when I *had* been a fish—no, billions and billions of fish, millions of generations of them over millions and millions of years. *Go back further,* I thought. I stopped swimming and let myself float. I was a single-celled animal now. *Further, further.* I was a leaf of seaweed. Trillions and trillions of leaves, I was the seaweed all over the world. Then I became the organic molecules that had evolved into seaweed. Then I was the minerals in the water, the dissolved salt . . . and then I was the water. A drop of pure water. A lake full of pure water. Stillness, pure, clear stillness. Then I was the—

"*AAAAAAAAAAAAAAAAAAA! SPLASH! AAAAAAA AAA! GASP COUGH GASP WHATSGOINGON-WHAT? WHO? WHEREAMI? WHE* . . . *OH* . . . *Oh* . . . *oh.* Oh. Sorry, man. What's going on?"

Somewhere around changing from a fish into kelp I had relaxed into a blissful dead man's float. Scott, as he had promised, was keeping a friendly eye on me. Time, being relative, made it appear to him that I had been floating like that for a long time, which led him into a bit of a reverie of his own where he imagined that I was one of the victims of the *Titanic*. When he finally remembered that it was me and that he was my Reality Park Ranger for the night, responsible for keeping me out of trouble, he thought he'd better tap me on the back to check on me. Imagine being all the water on earth one moment, and then feeling a tap. A tap where? *What's this?* Having a sensation at all came as a surprise to me, so it was understandable that I reacted so violently.

"I just had another lesson!" I spluttered to the best friend I'd ever had.

"Great, great! Why don't we, uh, go ashore now and you can tell me all about it." I think I might have spoiled Scott's lesson for the evening, because he seemed a bit subdued after that.

I told Scott the entire story of evolution from the point of view of someone who had been there. Then I told him the entire story of my life, marveling at the parallels between evolution on the macro and micro scales. I must have talked for quite a while because I noticed Scott shivering, and then I realized that our roaring campfire had burned down to nothing but embers. Then I noticed how dark it was. I'd never realized how dark darkness was until then, and yet I could see everything—how could I see everything? The leaves and trees—hey, they weren't in a perfect circle anymore. How the . . . ? Then I realized that it had been our campfire. It had lit the nearest leaves more brightly and the farther ones less so, which made it appear that we were in a bubble of foliage, when actually we were just in the bubble of light. Ah, of course. But still, how come I see it all now? Ah, the moonlight. Of course. I guessed that I was coming down.

Looking at the moon reminded me of astronomy, and I

looked beyond it to the stars. All those stars, so far away. So far away! The distances! THE DISTANCES! HERE WE GO AGAIN, OHMYGOD!

"SCOTT, DO YOU KNOW IF YOU COULD GET INTO A SPACESHIP AND DRIVE THROUGH SPACE AT FIFTY-FIVE MILES AN HOUR, HOW LONG IT WOULD TAKE YOU TO GET TO THE CLOSEST STAR?"

"Cool out! You don't have to yell, I'm right here! How long would it take?"

"Fifty-two million years!" I whispered.

"Whoa! How do you know that?"

"My dad's into astronomy."

"You don't have to whisper either, man, everything's cool."

"There are over a hundred billion galaxies in the universe! Think about that, man! That is like . . . that's just like, whoa! Man, Scott, I never understood the word 'whoa' before! Never like this!"

"Oh, yeah, weed *is* whoa, man. That's one of the first lessons."

"No no, it's not weed that's whoa, it's *this*! You know what I'm talking about? *This* experience. *This* moment, man! *Thisness!*"

"You're right! No, no, actually, *this* isn't whoa; it's that weed brings you and *this* together, and whoa is the state of consciousness that's the result. It's . . . I got it, it's the State of Whoa. Because all of this is mind, man, it's all mind. Like the Zen monks who were arguing, is it the flag moving, or is it the wind moving, and the Zen master came up and said, 'You're both wrong, you idiots, it's—"

"*Your mind moving!*" we said in perfect unison. He'd

read exactly the same Zen books I had! We were soul mates!

"*Whoa!*" we cried together, then laughed hysterically until our stomachs hurt.

As far as I was concerned, the evening was a success of infinite proportions. Inspired by my lengthy recitation of mind-bending astronomical facts, Scott told me about a book he'd read called *The Tao of Physics*. The book, he told me, was about subatomic particles, and how our Western scientists are only now having to acknowledge that Asian philosophers were right about the illusory nature of reality and the interconnectedness of everything, but the establishment just didn't want to acknowledge it. I couldn't wait to get my hands on that book and show it to my dad. I told Scott about the time my dad defended the "normal" modern, uptight state of mind as being perfectly natural because, he'd argued, anything that comes out of the brain is natural. Scott was impressed.

"Your dad's a cool guy," he said, nodding respectfully; "he's right about that." Then he stuck a finger in the air. "But he missed something there! Every state of mind is natural, which means that so is this one, so you can't say this is 'worse' than the uptight version. And if you had the freedom to choose, which you do, which would you choose?"

What would it be? The State of Whoa, or my dad's world—the State of Joe? The State of Whoa, man. It was so obvious. All my life I had wanted euphoria, intensity, a sense of fulfillment, of being completely engaged in life, and at last I'd found it.

"Uh . . . Mark?"

"Yeah?"

"Have you hit the lesson about hunger by any chance?"

"No, what lesson is that?"

"Lowlifes call it the munchies. It's when you gotta eat, man."

"No, man, I'm not hungry at all! Say, you want to know how long it would take to drive a car to the Globular Cluster in Hercules?"

"Uh, sure, but maybe on our next journey, OK? I gotta get something to eat. You OK to go home now?"

"Sure, no problem."

Scott and I shook hands—it was a profound handshake; so much was communicated without our saying anything—and parted. It was a profound parting, the way we turned and didn't look back even though we were still in each other's sight. I'd never realized how ritualistic parting was; you'd think people would always walk backward in order to see each other till the last possible moment, but they don't. Somewhere along the line cavemen had made the arbitrary decision to turn their backs when they parted and then they stuck to it because . . . well, actually, if they had walked backward, I realized, they couldn't have seen where they were going, and could have gotten hurt stumbling into a mammoth or something.

I walked home, every step a step closer to the place of my childhood, to my parents (they'd actually made me! Whoa!) and to my brother and sister. How I wanted to tell them all how much more I appreciated them now! When I reached the house I crept through it, looking at every piece of furniture, every musical instrument, every one of my dad's paintings and every photograph as if for the first time. This was where it had all begun. I could look at any object and instantly have a memory involving it flash into view. Everything was complete, everything had played an important part, everything was interconnected.

I went down into the basement and pulled out my cello. I started playing it, and I played as I never had before. Every note was perfect. I could do no wrong! I didn't have to bother with tempo or pitch at all; that was all in the past. This was the music of the spheres.

My door opened and I froze. "Mark, can I ask what the hell you're doing?" It was Dad.

"I . . . uh . . ."

"It's three o'clock in the morning, Mark. Do you mind?"

"Sorry, sorry . . ."

I lay down and closed my eyes. For some reason I remembered a poster that a childhood friend of mine had in his bedroom. It read: TODAY IS THE TOMORROW YOU WORRIED ABOUT YESTERDAY. NOW YOU KNOW WHY.

The words whirled around in my head and rearranged themselves, with a few changes along the way, then appeared in front of me like this: TODAY IS THE TOMORROW I WISHED FOR YESTERDAY. NOW I KNOW WHY. I'd really SEEN. And the best part of it was that I could go to sleep with utter peace of mind, knowing that I had not gone crazy, had not gotten caught and was not going to become an addict, because I knew I would never have to do it again. Now that I had SEEN this way, and now that I UNDERSTOOD so much, it could never be taken away from me.

14

The next day I woke up around one in the afternoon. I went upstairs, made some toast and sat in the living room. I felt kind of crappy. My mother passed by me without looking at me. Oh my God, could she tell? Did she know? I told myself not to panic, that she was just annoyed that I'd gotten up so late. Our rule since I'd turned sixteen was that on weekends, because I stayed up much later than she did, she had to wait until I'd gotten up on my own before going down to practice.

"Where's Dad?" I asked her. I had all sorts of new theories about the origins of the universe that I wanted to run past him. He didn't have to know exactly how the theories had been inspired.

"Joe is uptown getting oil. First he had to go to the dump, then he has to change the oil in both cars, then he has to mow the lawn."

The subtext, communicated via the tension in her voice,

was that Dad had been working all morning while I was sleeping. If I didn't get up off my ass and start doing something helpful fast, I was going to be in the doghouse all weekend. In spite of having passed from the ordinary sad world into the Incomparable State of Whoa only a few hours before, I was feeling strangely grouchy. Instead of taking her cue and offering to do some chore, or at least reassuring her by practicing some classical music for a change instead of spending *all* my time doodling in G major, I stomped out of the house and sat in the dead Triumph.

Wait a minute, I thought, this is ridiculous. Didn't I leave this bullshit behind me? What happened to the State of Whoa? I closed my eyes and tried to bring it back, but failed. I was back in the State of Joe, except that it was a bit worse than usual because my head ached. As I sat there in the rusting car, marveling at how difficult it was to concentrate on anything, my dad pulled into the driveway. I felt happy to see him; I was looking forward to an afternoon of metaphysical discussion. Maybe then I would slip back into the proper frame of mind.

But as soon as he climbed out of the bus I could see he wasn't in any mood for metaphysics. He hated driving uptown, he hated changing the oil and he hated mowing the lawn. Maybe I should offer to mow the lawn for him, I thought. But then I remembered how fatigued and headachy I felt and decided, no, I think I'll go down to the lake.

I found the ashes of our campfire from the night before. It was hard to believe this was the same spot that had been so magical; everything looked so disappointingly ordinary. I tried wading into the water, but my feet were unusually sensitive to the sharp sand, the slimy algae and the beer-bottle caps. And the water was cold and kind of dirty. I tried to retrace the steps of my insights, beginning with the fish experience, but instead of tapping into my genetically encoded memories, I felt cold and self-conscious.

I walked around the neighborhood and everything bothered me in the same way. The sounds of lawn mowers, the bits of discarded paper, plastic and metal along the side of the road, the muggy weather, the mosquitoes, the flies, the smell of asphalt and even the trees. The trees all looked so . . . so bland. Why couldn't we have anything really unusual like palm trees or Monterey pines? Why did I have to spend my whole life in *Connecticut?*

Bummer. I never really knew the meaning of that word until now. It wasn't worth it; this was too depressing. I vowed never to mess with dope again.

The next day I felt better and went back to my routine of playing along to the stereo in the afternoon and going out at night. As the days passed, my memories of "the day after" began to fade, whereas my curiosity about Whoaness increased. After two weeks it was all I could think about. I couldn't see any reason why the intellectual perspective couldn't be transferred into one's normal, sober life. Maybe if I got stoned and made that the subject of my mental explorations, I could use my superior powers of insight to figure out how to make the transfer. Good idea! Once more couldn't hurt, and as Mr. Leighton implied in the conversation we'd never had in the faculty lounge, teenagers almost have to sacrifice a few brain cells on their path to adulthood—it's been a universal rite of passage since the dawn of mankind, hasn't it? The wise Native Americans, after all, made their youths fast for days, sit in overheated saunas, hang themselves from bloody hooks passed through their chests or chew mescal buttons in order to have the kind of hallucinations deemed necessary for the passage to adulthood. You can bet those noble braves lost a few neurons along the way, boy.

I spoke to Scott about it and asked if he could give me enough pot for just one more lesson. He obliged, so I stopped by Ye Olde Head Shoppe, picked up a little pipe and some matches, and drove straight out to the lake to get things right.

WHOA! HOW COULD I HAVE FORGOTTEN *THIS?* IT'S SO SIMPLE, SO OBVIOUS, SO UNDENI-ABLE, SO PERMANENT!

Bummer. I'll never do this again.

But I did, and then a fourth time, and then I decided that it must be like medication for depression; you had to do it steadily over a certain period of time before it really sank in. Whoa! Bummer. Whoa! Bummer. Whoa! Bummer.

The summer of '76 was all Whoa! Bummer. Then fall. That first week when Erich and Rachel went off to school but I stayed at home, I felt strange. I had expected it to be a joyous occasion, but instead, whenever I drove by the high school on my way to town to meet Scott for a pizza lunch, I felt slightly anxious. Did I really know what I was doing? Meanwhile, every day my brother would come home and tell me that at the end of the morning announcements, a crisp female voice would say, "And will Mark Salzman please report to the main office immediately. Mark Salzman." Ah, bureaucracy.

I was still practicing jazz in the afternoons, but was getting stoned every night. Worries that I might be getting addicted troubled me every now and then, but were easily

177

silenced by the argument that once I had figured out the essential psychological ingredients of Whoaness and learned to invoke them without smoking pot, I would be glad I had not surrendered to fear and given up. And I *was* trying, too; I set aside a certain part of every afternoon to take a walk and try to think myself into that state of mind, but without success. As to precautions against getting caught, I didn't take many. At first I took my pipe out to the backyard and smoked it there, but after a while I smoked right in the basement and burned lots of incense to mask it.

One day Lenny called me up to say that he'd bought a Triumph Spitfire but had totaled it after only two weeks. But he had an idea: we could take what was left of his car and what was left of mine and pool the parts, building one composite car that ran. We could share it; one week it would be his, the next week mine. Great idea! We towed my car over to his front yard and got things started on the right foot by setting up his eight-track tape player out on the grass, blasting some Pink Floyd and lighting up a bowl of Colombian.

Nine days later we had one car, but three pails of nuts and bolts that should somehow have gone into the car but hadn't. What the fuck! (That was our project motto.) We started up the car and decided to take it out to a nearby stretch of flat road built over a shallow swamp where we could test it out. When we reached the road Lenny stopped. "Let's see how fast it goes from zero to sixty," he suggested. He revved the engine, popped the clutch, and in less than a second we discovered where some of those nuts and bolts should have gone. We had forgotten to bolt the steering column (which on a Spitfire is just a thin metal pole) to the wheel apparatus, and we had forgotten to bolt the seats down; the acceleration threw us both back, the steering wheel pulled right back with us and the car roared right into the swamp. Luckily it was a convertible. As we lay on our backs and felt the car sink, Lenny said, "What the fuck?"

A friend helped us pull the car out and tow it back to his place. Within a week we had it together again, but on his first night out solo with it Lenny wrapped it around a tree. A few days later we were working on it again when, just as I was switching the tape from the Eagles to the Who, a nondescript car stopped in front of Lenny's house and two men in suits walked up to us. One of them asked if either of us was Lenny.

"Yeah," Lenny said.

Flashing a badge, the man identified himself as a detective and read Lenny his rights. Neither of the men looked at me or asked me anything.

"You're kidding me," Lenny finally said.

"You know we don't kid around," the detective answered. They put Lenny into the car and drove away with him, and that was the end of our Triumph repair project. I never did find out what the arrest was about.

Lenny's problem should have been a warning to me that I was headed for trouble. Here I was, accepted by Yale but hanging around all day getting stoned, listening to bands like Ten Years After and tinkering with shitty British sports cars. I didn't read the signs, though. I was under the impression that I was getting dramatically better as a jazz cellist every day, but in fact I was still playing the same three songs with Scott, and we rarely played for longer than an hour at a time before going out to the woods to do our really important work, which was smoking dope and being Amazed by Everything.

In time I solved the bummer problem by being constantly high. I ate, drank, talked, slept, hung out with Annette, played the cello, bussed tables and looked through the telescope just as I had done in my previous life; only now all of my experiences seemed part of a vast, profound, mysterious but slightly blurry adventure.

As far as saving money for college went, I wasn't building up much of a nest egg. I got fed up with the Sri Chinmoy people; they were always smiling, but that was probably because they were paying me well below minimum wage. I quit that job and got hired by the wife of a wealthy executive to paint Chinese-landscape paintings directly on several of the interior walls of their house. They had two French exchange students staying with them, both girls, but I never got to see their faces because they spent every day upstairs in their room listening to the Beatles' song "Michelle" and singing along to the French lyrics.

When I finished that job I got a check for five hundred dollars. I took it to my bank to cash it so I could buy another car—this time one that would run—but the check bounced. I was furious. When I called the family from the bank, there was no answer. Seeing that there was a problem, the manager of the bank came over and when he saw who had written the check, said, "Oh, yeah, I talked to them this morning. They're on their way to the Caribbean." He authorized the check and handed me the money, but only after first calling me "miss" (older guys loved pulling the "I thought you were a girl" routine on me when my hair was long), then giving me a frowning lecture about being impatient. I, who was completely broke, got written a bad check for a month's work by a couple of millionaires on their way to the beach, and *I* get a lecture about being impatient. That's teenage life.

That afternoon I went out to buy the car I'd chosen. This time it was a Triumph TR4, and the man who sold it to me swore it ran great. "Burns a little oil," he said, "but nothing to worry about." This time my father drove behind me in the Volkswagen to make sure I got home OK. Halfway home smoke started pouring out of the engine. We pulled over to the side of the Merritt Parkway for a quick conference.

"I don't care what you do with this thing, Mark, but we'd better get it off the parkway quick," Dad said; we didn't have temporary plates on it and he didn't want to get fined or arrested.

I hopped back in but the car wouldn't start. Dad stuck his head out the window and said, "Put it in gear. Let's get the hell out of here." I did so and he drove up to my rear bumper and pushed until the damn thing started.

It was the longest half-hour drive of my life. Smoke was pouring out so thick I thought the whole thing might catch on fire at any moment. When we got it home I shut the engine off but the smoke didn't stop; it *was* on fire! By the time I got the flames out the engine was ruined.

I called the man who'd sold it to me and he said he didn't know anything about it; it was his son's car and his son was in the marines, and anyhow, if I ruined the engine, it was my problem. So my second car ended up just like the first one—in the weeds at the end of the driveway.

Later that year Lenny resurfaced and called to say he was trying to put together a field trip to New York City to go see Laserium, the music-and-light show in the old Hayden

Planetarium building. He had another car now, a tiny four-door Datsun, that he said he'd modified just for this trip. I was up for it; I didn't have to get up early for anything the next day.

As the car came up my street the first thing I noticed was the music; Lenny had put his eight-track in there and Dark Side of the Moon was on full blast. The next thing I noticed as he pulled into the driveway was that I couldn't see him, or for that matter anyone in the car; it looked as if the windows had all been sprayed with dull white paint. When the car stopped, the driver's-side door opened, Lenny stepped out and billows of smoke poured out after him. "Hop in!" he cried, grinning like the Cheshire cat.

I climbed into the passenger side and took a whiff. It was dope, of course. He'd put a huge water pipe in the glove compartment and rigged four tubes along the inside of the roof so the driver and each passenger had his own private mouthpiece. I turned around and waved the smoke a bit to have a look at the passengers in the backseat. There were Scott and Michael.

I was mighty surprised to see Michael in there, and he looked surprised to see me. We didn't say a thing to each other. There was a certain tension in the air when Lenny told us to get the water pipe going because neither Michael nor I wanted to be the one seen by the other smoking pot. Finally he shrugged, took a drag off the pipe and the tension was broken.

Someone ought to do a survey someday to find out if the Laserium show has ever actually been witnessed by a sober person. You wouldn't think so from the look, sound and smell of the audience I saw it with. Halfway through the show one guy started bellowing out, "I SEE GOD! I SEE HIM! THERE HE IS! THERE HE IS!" and had to be led out by two ushers. I wasn't impressed by the show, to be honest. A couple of little dots going in circles to lame songs like "Dreamweaver"—Scott and I had done that with penlights in his room a hundred times already, and we used better music. All four of us were disappointed. We started walking back to the car, then stopped at a coffee shop for a snack before the long drive back to Connecticut. Michael and I still hadn't said anything to each other.

Full of doughnuts and coffee, we went back out to find our car, but after going up and down streets for half an hour, we realized that not one of us had been paying attention when we parked it. We had no idea where it was, and within a short amount of time we had no idea where Laserium had been either. We wandered for a long time. Michael complained that he had to go to the bathroom. After a fruitless search for a public bathroom he unzipped his pants in front of a fire hydrant and let loose. It was the longest piss I've ever heard; I was sure the NYPD would catch us.

By the time we found the car all of us had come down and were in a terrible mood. We lit up the pipe once we got onto the interstate and started to feel better when all of a sudden the car started to slow down, then stopped.

"This is so fucked up," Lenny said. "I forgot to put gas in it this morning."

We were on a dark stretch of I-95 just outside of Rye, New York.

"We'll have to push it," Michael said, even though we were at least thirty miles from home.

"Oh, man, this is so fucked up," Lenny kept saying.

Scott pushed on the passenger-side door while Michael and I put our shoulders against the trunk and dug in for the long haul. It was a light car, three of us were pushing, and we must have been on a slight downward slope, because in no time at all we were really moving.

"Push harder, candy-ass!" Michael yelled at me, starting to laugh. "You're not pushing at all!"

"What are you talking about? You're the one not pushing! I see you resting your head on the trunk!"

"Resting, my ass! I'm having to make up for the fact that you've got nothing in your legs anymore! Look at you! You're already out of breath!"

"And you're not breathing hard at all, no!"

We were talking at last. As badly as I wanted to get home and get to bed, I was glad we were friends again.

"Look! An exit!" Scott yelled. We pushed the car off the ramp, then all jumped on top of it as it picked up speed and coasted to the bottom, where an all-night Exxon station was waiting for us. The car rolled right up to the pump.

We filled the tank, but when the time came to pay we all started fumbling around in our pockets and realized that none of us had a cent. We'd spent it all on that stupid laser show and doughnuts.

"This is so fucked up," Lenny kept saying.

"What are we gonna do now?" Scott asked.

Michael smiled and said, "You can all relax. I've been in a situation like this once before, and let me tell you that we are lucky men tonight because we have in our midst the perfect man to get us on our way. Gentlemen," he said, gesturing toward me with a vaguely Arabian, spiral flourish of his hand, "meet Barabbas, the Christian Thief."

"How am I gonna get us out of this?" I asked.

"Remember the drive-in movie? You go in there and do your magic. Confess, and free us all!"

I walked into the station, where an unhappy guy in his late thirties was shivering and watching a portable black-and-white television set. It was 4:00 A.M.

"You guys better have money," he said.

"Um . . . here's what happened. We went down to New York to see Laserium, we lost our car, and it's been the worst night of any of our lives. If I give you my driver's license, can I come back in a couple of hours and pay you back?"

He squinted at me and then at the car. "Did you say Laserium?" he asked.

"Yeah, have you seen it?"

"Yep. You guys got any dope?"

I hesitated.

"You give me a couple joints, I'll take care of the gas."

When I came back to the car the guys were looking at me expectantly. I simply smiled, got into the car and said, "We're cool. Let's go."

Michael gave me a friendly slap across the back. "What'd I tell you guys?" he roared. "We weren't the judo-jitsi brothers for nothing."

I was glad to have seen Michael that night, but couldn't bring myself to call him after that, and he didn't call me. I wasn't all that comfortable with the sight of him, once so pure but now smoking pot and pissing on fire hydrants in Manhattan, and I'm sure he felt the same way about me. We didn't renew our friendship.

Not long after Laserium I made a truly glaring error of judgment—the sort of error that only someone stoned most of the day could make, and that everyone who is stoned most of the day eventually does make—and that was deciding to grow my own dope in my parents' house. I started a dozen seedlings in an egg carton on the windowsill of my room, but then I thought, Sooner or later, Mom or Dad is going to wonder what these plants are. So I decided that, since my dad enjoyed houseplants and had them growing all over the house, I would put one seedling in each of his pots and that way, spread around like that, my plants would blend in and no one would notice them. This would also save me the trouble of remembering to water them; given my permanent citizenship in the State of Whoa, remembering anything was a real challenge.

The plants got about six inches high when one evening after dinner but before dessert, my brother, Erich, wandered up to the table with the *World Book*—Volume "M"—under his arm. He plunked it down on the table and opened it to "Marijuana." Innocently pointing to the large photo of a typical cannabis leaf, he said, "Isn't this weird? This picture looks just like the little plants that have been coming up in a bunch of Dad's pots."

Mom was in the kitchen, out of earshot. Dad looked at the photo, then got up quietly and examined his little pots. I sat paralyzed with horror at the dinner table. It had honestly never occurred to me that he might recognize them, or that any of the parents of Mom's thirty music students who sat next to the plants for half an hour at a time each week might recognize them. Now that this had happened, I felt as if my entire soul were imploding. I felt *really, really stupid.*

Dad didn't say a word. Part of his self-control, I believe, came from the fact that my mother had an important concert to give the next day and he didn't want her to know about this until after her concert. He came back to the table and looked at me in a way that said, "You are not the person I thought you were. I'm not sure I even know you. All I know is, I want those plants out of my house *right now.*"

I got the message. I got up and one by one pulled my plants up and threw them out into the woods. I didn't dare go back into the house until after nightfall, and even then I slinked down to my room without talking to anyone.

The next day my father and I had to move the harpsichord to the concert hall together. It was a heavy and somewhat delicate job, and took lots of teamwork; usually I enjoyed doing it with him, but this time it was hell. I felt nauseated and had a splitting headache, both from being tense and having not slept at all the night before. Neither of us said a word.

We delivered the harpsichord and Mom gave her concert. Dad didn't sit in the hall. He stayed outside, and I wasn't about to go looking for him. After the concert we dismantled the harpsichord and carried it into the van. He was ashen-faced and never once looked me in the eye. Halfway home Dad said the only thing he was ever to say about The Incident: "I hope you don't ruin your life." Something about the way he said the words "your life" made me think, He doesn't just mean my life this week or this month—he means my whole life, forever, eternity, until I die. Until I die in that damp alley in New York City, just like the elementary school drug film said I would.

When we got home I went out to the woods behind the house and threw up. That was when I began to lose interest in smoking dope.

15

Two days after The Incident I sneaked out to the woods where I had thrown the little marijuana seedlings and tried to recover them in case they were good for smoking. As I crawled around miserably in the bushes it occurred to me how pathetic I must look, and that was when I hit my low point. Just as the policeman who visited our sixth-grade class had warned us after letting us all touch his pistol, I had let myself slip—a tiny bit at first, but sure enough, I had set the wheels of self-destruction in motion. I had started down that infamous road to ruin as sure as if I had set fire to the Town Hall, thrown a rock through the plate-glass window at Woolworth's or stuffed rags up the sheriff's exhaust pipe. I had become a Bad Kid. I had ruined my relationship with my parents forever. I had wasted half a year celebrating banal insights and playing the same stolen electric-bass riffs over and over without actually learning any of the essentials of real improvisation, and I couldn't even do full splits anymore. After all the opportunities I'd been handed, what had I made of it all? Where had I ended up? Scrounging around in the woods for a couple of limp hallucinogenic twigs. I was ashamed of myself, and convinced that my dad needn't have bothered to worry; I had already ruined my life.

I looked over to the driveway and saw the inert hulk of the TR4. I couldn't even buy a car that worked! A feeling of rage came over me with such force that I charged at the stupid Triumph, picked up a cinder block and before I knew it I had completely demolished the car. When my arms were too tired to lift the cinder block anymore I aimed a series of hopping side kicks at the doors and fenders, and found that, Michael's comment to the contrary, I still had enough in my legs to dent metal pretty good. My mother was in the house while I was having my little temper tantrum, and she must have heard it all, but when I went back indoors an hour or so later she didn't say anything. She hated the Triumph too, so maybe she sensed I was heading in a good direction.

When Dad came home from work and saw the car, however, he had quite a bit to say about it. He looked at me hard across the table and said, "I thought you were supposed to be working to save money for college this year. What happened to that, huh?"

I knew this wasn't one of those questions I was supposed to answer.

"I'll tell you what happened. You've done a couple of odd jobs, and then you've gone out and wasted the money on two fancy-looking pieces of crap that anybody with half a brain could have told you wouldn't run. You could have bought yourself a reliable car easily, but no, you had to be special. You weren't going to drive some ordinary car that an ordinary kid would drive. You're so smart and talented that you had to have a snazzy convertible so everybody would know how different you were from the pack. Then, when they don't run, you sulk, push them five feet down the driveway and let them rust on my lawn. Now you decide to destroy one. That's just great, Mark; that's so smart I don't know what to say."

The most terrifying part about this speech was not that he was angry; I expected at least that. The scary thing was that he was being sarcastic. He had never made bitter, sarcastic remarks about any of us kids, ever. It was uncharacteristic of him.

"Now," Dad continued, "I have a beat-up rusted-out car in my yard, broken glass all over the driveway, and the front hood, I notice, is ten yards away in a drainage ditch. Thanks so much for the landscaping touches. Now, what I want to know is, what's going to happen when at the end of this year you don't have enough money to go to Yale? You want to spend another year sitting around on your ass playing that . . . that *bullshit*? I certainly hope not, because your mother and I both are getting real sick of hearing those same, repetitive, twiddly-diddly-dwee dee-dwee dee-dwee songs over and over again, and having to climb over you when you're asleep until noon, and then having to go to bed every night wondering if you've crashed the car. Enough is enough. I've got news for you, pal, you're getting a job, and you're getting it tomorrow. A woman where I work has a husband who's a lawyer, and his building needs someone in the mail room. You are going to get a haircut first thing tomorrow morning; then you are going to drive Mom's car to Greenwich and have an interview with that lawyer at three o'clock. Here's the address." He handed me a slip of paper, got up and went into the living room to watch the news.

It was horrible having to sit through all this, but I was too tired from smashing the car to act indignant. And anyway, I agreed with him. The next morning I went straight to the first barbershop I could find; it was the first time in about four years that I'd had a haircut, and the first time I'd ever chosen the barbershop myself. The old guy took one look at my hair, which reached down practically to my belt, and started laughing. "Can I help you, miss?" he asked, smiling unpleasantly.

"I have a job interview at a lawyer's office in like four hours. I need a haircut."

His face brightened considerably. "You got an interview with a lawyer today? Oh, this is gonna be sweet. Any chair you like, son."

When I stood up and looked in the mirror ten minutes later I almost passed out; I looked twelve years old. On the other hand, no one would be calling me "miss" anymore.

I drove to Greenwich and found the address. It was a historic but decaying four-story building with an elevator run by a cheerful old Swiss janitor. He showed me where to go for my interview.

I met with the lawyer, Mr. Shaw, and to my intense relief he was friendly and casual. He mentioned what a nice guy my dad was, and how highly his wife always spoke of his work. People always spoke highly of my dad's work, and apparently none of them knew how much he hated the job. The lawyer told me how excited he was for me that I was going to be going to such a great school, how many good things he and his wife had heard about me, and what a pleasure it would be to have me working for his firm for nine months or so. Maybe I could come back every summer? I realized that he hadn't heard about my true identity as a total shit. At one point in the interview he cocked his head to one side and said, "Only one thing: I thought I heard you had really long hair. I was expecting hair down to your ankles or something."

"I got it cut this morning for this interview."

His face broke up and he struggled to keep from laughing. "You're kidding! You didn't have to do that, for heaven's sake! You'll be down in the mail room most of the day; you won't have to impress the little old ladies with blue hair and poodles the way I do! Did your dad make you do that?"

"Yeah."

"What a guy, that Joe!" He allowed himself a chuckle. Yeah. What a guy.

I started the next day. Dad woke me up at six, we had some breakfast, then began the freezing-cold drive south to Greenwich. It was exactly an hour each way, and Volkswagen buses have never been much prized for their heating systems.

Fortunately it was a beautiful drive through some of the prettiest scenery in Connecticut and New York State. That first morning we drove past a crystal-clear reservoir that reflected the orange glow in the eastern sky like a mirror. Right in the center of the reservoir, the mirror was disturbed by a single duck paddling across the water, and the ripples it left behind it created a surreal pattern of orange and blue stripes. Dad pulled the car off to the side of the road so he could take a few pictures. This was how he got his ideas for paintings, trying to keep his mind off work by watching the scenery carefully as he drove. When he saw something he might like to use later, he stopped the car, hopped out and took a picture of it.

Although I had been dreading the first silent drive to work with my dad after The Incident, and felt anxious about the new job, I was actually enjoying being up so early in the morning. I felt clearheaded, and at least I wasn't being caught doing anything bad. As Dad dropped me off at the building, he said, "Good luck." At least he was speaking to me again.

One other boy and I were to replace the two retired policemen who had run the mail room for about ten years. The two ex-cops made a perfect match; one was the straight guy, the other the joker. When I met the first cop, I noticed he had a terrible wound on his forehead. It looked awful, as if it were either a deep, permanent black bruise or maybe a metal plate just under the skin. Then I met the second cop, and he had an identical wound on his forehead! Maybe they had both gotten shot on the same assignment, which was why they still worked together, I thought. Or maybe they had met in rehab and formed a bond. But on my second day, I noticed to my surprise that both of them had healed completely. I asked someone about it and she told me, "They're Irish, silly! Yesterday was Ash Wednesday. Haven't you ever seen a Catholic before? That was ash rubbed on their heads."

The other boy hired with me, Marty Schiff, was a riot. He could do all the Monty Python skits by heart, with the proper accents; he told great jokes and he made incredibly funny faces. I took to him instantly, but I started to notice on the second day that he seemed distracted all the time and I was forever having to cover his small mistakes. On the third day he left the firm's mailbox at the post office wide open; I got an anxious call from the post office. They had closed the box right away, but didn't know how long it had been left open. I ran at full speed all the way down the street to deal with it. The postal worker who had discovered the problem was not amused, and assumed that it was I who had left it open. "Jesus Christ, anybody could have just reached in and pulled out some old lady's life savings in negotiable bonds! Are you nuts or something? You're lucky I'm in a good mood today," he warned, "or you'd be out of a job. What's your name?"

I told him. "Yeah, well, I'll be watching you, Mr. Salzman." God, not this again. I'd had enough of being in trouble.

I took the rap without squealing, but went back to the mail room really angry. When I told my colleague what had happened, he started laughing.

"I guess it's 'cause I'm tripping!" he announced, his eyes wide and bloodshot, and then he went into another giggling fit.

"What are you tripping on?" I asked.

"The best acid you ever heard of! You want a tab?"

How quickly the tables had turned! Fucking drug addict, I thought. Not in *my* mail room you don't. But what was I going to do? I wanted to talk to my dad about it, but given my recent circumstances I didn't think that would be a good idea. I tossed and turned all weekend. On Monday the fellow showed up an hour late, and when he had to deliver a document he got lost and disappeared for the rest of the morning and I got yelled at for this by the office manager, a lonely woman who came back from lunch every day drunk and who insisted on calling me "Marx."

It was a horrible situation. No one likes to snitch, but I wasn't prepared to follow that guy around and worry about taking the rap all the time. But I didn't want to tell the office manager because I wasn't sure she was operating on all cylinders; besides, she couldn't tell the two of us apart. The chances were about even that I would be the one she fired. I took a big risk and went up to see Mr. Shaw, the lawyer who had interviewed me. I didn't say that my co-worker was an LSD freak, and I didn't tell him about the open mailbox, but I did mention the smaller mistakes and said that I was worried about Marty's ability to concentrate. I said I hated being in this position but that I desperately needed this job and didn't want to be blamed for somebody else's mistakes and get fired.

Mr. Shaw nodded and said, "We're already aware that Marty is, shall we say, under the weather. Somebody found him yesterday down in the file basement having a fairly animated conversation with a spiderweb. But you know, once you hire somebody you have to be careful about how you handle things like this. You have to give the person the benefit of the doubt. He might just be the creative type. I'm sorry you've had to worry about this, but let's be patient. If he settles in and gets the hang of things soon, great, but if not, let me worry about it, not you. You're doing fine, and I promise that nobody's going to blame you for anything you haven't done, just as we won't rush to any conclusions about Marty."

What a relief, and how impressed I was by how he handled it. This was one cool head. From then on I relaxed, and before long I realized that I had mastered the simple tasks of the job. To my surprise, I discovered not only that I could do the job well, but that I enjoyed it. In fact, I loved it. The first thing in the morning I went down to the post office, unlocked the firm's mailbox and filled my canvas sack with all the mail, making sure to wave confidently at the postal worker who had his eye on me.

Back at the firm I sorted all the correspondence into a floor-to-ceiling rack, then put it all in order in a tray and made my first rounds, starting at the fourth floor and working my way down. Each attorney had at least one secretary, and most of my contact was with them. I would hand each of them a little pile of mail and take whatever they had for me to send out. I liked it when they had emergencies and needed something hand-delivered immediately because it broke up the routine. I took it as a challenge to try to run so fast to my destination that no one noticed I had been out.

I also liked timing each routine task to see if I could come up with ways to shave a few seconds off the time it took. Why not? Some people might think it stupid to try to finish a mindless task early because then you'll get assigned other mindless tasks, but I discovered within a few days that time flies much faster when you are concentrating hard, so as far as I was concerned, give me all the mindless tasks you've got. There was a certain irony in this discovery; for years I'd put myself through all kinds of exotic mental and physical training in order ultimately to be able to do even the most menial tasks with an alert mind, and I had failed. Now I was running a mail room in Greenwich and succeeding without any philosophical guidance at all. I did not admit this to my father, however.

Before long I felt as if most of the secretaries in the building were either my older sisters or my aunts, and I enjoyed spending a few minutes at each one's desk hearing their news and discovering the underrated pleasure of small talk. High on their list was speculating about whether or not the police would ever catch the "Son of Sam" killer, and complaining about the lawyers. If I had extra time on slow days, I liked coming up with little surprises; sometimes I went up the street to the ice-cream shop, where the owner, who got lots of business from those secretaries, would make up a box with thirty tiny cups of ice cream in it at no charge; then I would rush back and try to drop the cups off for everybody before they melted.

Something that I had never imagined when I pictured myself having a job was how bearable drudgery can be when it is shared. Most of the people I dealt with—people who did the filing, secretarial and janitorial work in office buildings, probate buildings, city halls and police stations, along with the people who worked in the restaurants, bars and supply houses that supported those office workers—were surprisingly cheerful. Within a couple of weeks I looked back on my life as a full-time Student of Alternative Reality, spraying my mouth with Binaca all the time, pouring Murine into my eyes and playing the cello badly along with Weather Report albums, and wondered how I could ever have thought that this was the way to live.

Marty, alas, never did get the hang of the job. One Monday morning when I showed up, the office manager introduced me to Ed, my new co-worker, whom I would be training "as of right now. Ed, this is Marx."

Ed was an older guy, overweight, and diabetes was making him lose his sight. He was in a permanent bad mood, he had permanent bad breath, and he didn't like being trained by a kid. He especially didn't like being trained by a kid who enjoyed the challenge of menial tasks; we had deeply conflicting philosophies about work. He liked sitting back in his squeaky chair, scratching his huge balls—which were always on display since he wore cheap, form-fitting doubleknit pants and sat with his legs splayed as wide open as they would go—and saying, "Mark, someday you'll figure it out. You'll figure out the secret to life, and to working for people like this. You're a nice kid, but you're naive. You're a fresh-faced, naive kid. You wanna know what the secret is? I'll save you some time and tell ya." He would lean forward, stick his face right into mine, and whisper, "Fuck 'em!" then give the finger to all the condescending, rich, white-collar para-sites upstairs. This was the secret.

Ed was lazy, but he wasn't on acid and he could be good company sometimes. God, he was slow, though. I believe that he timed himself during routine tasks to see if he could find ways to *add on* a few seconds here and there, and whenever someone asked him to make an emergency delivery he would wince and say, "You know, I really hate it when you people act like we've got nothing to do down here. You just assume we should just jump up at your beck and command. Why didn't this come down on the regular mail run? That's what it's for, you know. You people put this stuff off until the last minute, then expect us down in the trenches to run off like good little bunnies and fix it for you." Most of the secretaries didn't want to get into a confrontation, so they would soothe him with self-deprecatory remarks and promise that in the future they'd try harder to give him advance warning. But it was never the secretary's fault that there was an emergency; the lawyer had handed her the envelope only minutes before. It usually wasn't the lawyer's fault either; he'd probably gotten the call from some distressed client only a few minutes before *that*. It wasn't anyone's fault; it was the job. It was a law firm, for God's sake, and lawyers deal with crises.

When the secretary left, Ed would toss the envelope on

the desk, wink at me and say, "Fuck 'em!" and when I could stand it no longer I would go make his delivery. He would laugh and say, "See, Mark? There's always some fresh-faced kid out there who doesn't know the secret who'll run around for you. You'll figure it out someday, fresh-face!"

Ed sometimes got annoyed with me, but he liked me overall and took a sort of paternal interest in my romantic life. When he found out I'd had a steady girlfriend for a year he thought that was silly. "You don't go out with one girl when you're seventeen, Mark. You gotta play the field." He wasn't at all inhibited by the fact that he hadn't had a date since World War II. When he heard that I was still a virgin he practically fell over in his chair.

"Jesus!" he yelled, roaring with laughter, "seventeen years old in this day and age and he hasn't gotten laid yet? Oh, Christ, Mark! If when I was your age I knew what I know now, I'd be getting laid every night with a different girl! I could have any girl I wanted!" He snapped his fingers for emphasis.

Ed never specified exactly what it was that he didn't know then but did know now beyond saying, "All ya gotta do is know what to say, and when to say it. That's all ya gotta do, fresh-face." He even bought me a pack of rubbers to put in my wallet in case I got lucky someday.

Working full-time made me realize that if I wanted to keep up with music I had to be more disciplined about my practice time. I talked with my mother about it, and delighted that I was asking her advice, she suggested that what I needed was a concrete goal to work toward. There was a youth music competition coming up in a month, she said; if I wanted to give it a try, I would have to prepare one required movement of Bach and one piece of my own choice. Since I had not had a formal cello lesson in almost four years, and it wouldn't be fair to start with a new teacher just for the competition, she would do her best to coach me. I would have to practice at night—every night.

I decided to give it a go. The next day my dad mentioned on our commute that I'd better take the competition seriously; all of the judges knew Mom, so in a way her reputation was at stake. She was the one signing the entry form as my sponsor, saying that she thought I was qualified and wouldn't be wasting the judges' time.

My mother's reputation! Talk about pressure. I decided to keep my chosen piece a surprise from everyone until the competition. I started practicing steadily at night, but that still didn't give me enough time, so I took to waking up at five and doing quiet scales before breakfast. There *still* wasn't enough time, so I started bringing my cello to work every day. I kept it down in the file basement, and instead of going out for lunch I brought a sandwich down there and practiced.

My mother tried to help me with the Bach, but the truth was that I didn't spend nearly enough time on it; I was really focusing on my optional piece. She tried several times to warn me that I would regret not having the Bach in better shape, but I didn't, or couldn't, listen. "I just hope you remember that this is a *classical* music competition," she said when I insisted on keeping my optional piece a secret. Oh, it's classical, I assured her.

Somehow I made it to the finals. That Sunday afternoon we finalists had to play our required *and* our chosen piece on a stage in front of the judges, and the auditorium was open to the public. Annette and even a bunch of my Laserium buddies—except for Michael—had come to cheer me on. I came out and played the Bach . . . badly. Then I walked offstage, tore off my jacket and shirt, put on Annette's Nehrudelic outfit, brought my cello out and laid it across my lap. I could see my mother closing her eyes.

I'd prepared a morning raga, a piece of *classical* Indian music. At least I can say that I played it better than I had the Bach. When I finished all my friends started yelling "Encore!" and "Eat a peach for Duane Allman!" and held their pocket lighters up in the air as if it were a rock concert.

Miraculously, I took second place. The winner was a boy whose eyeline barely reached up to my belt. It was a bit of a letdown having to stand next to this toddler while he got the bigger trophy, but he deserved the prize; that kid was something. That night my parents were actually in a good mood over something I had done, and it came as a gigantic relief to me.

A few days later my mother handed me an envelope. "It's the judges' remarks," she said. "I always look at them because there's usually at least one helpful critical comment there." I didn't really want to read criticism, but curiosity got the better of me. There were five judges, only one of them a cellist. The four noncellists all had polite things to say about the Bach, but it was obviously the raga that had won them over; in fact, they had given me such high marks for it that it seemed I should have gotten first prize rather than second. When I read the cellist's sheet, however, my face turned red with shame.

"The second piece was not cello playing," he scrawled, "so I can't comment on it. The Bach was a mess. Dreadful left-hand technique, no bow control at all. Possibly musical, but how can you tell through that disastrous technique? Scratchy sound, squeaks, weak tone, etc." In each category he had given me the lowest possible numerical score except for "Originality." He was pretty generous there.

I showed it to my mother and she froze. At first I didn't know what was going on, but then I realized that she was furious. "Who is this?" she fumed, her hands shaking with rage. She tore the sheet out of my hand and looked at his name. "William Turner . . ." she read aloud. "I'll find out who this is and I'll write him a letter and tell him exactly what I think of this! Nobody has the right to say such mean things about you! Nobody!" Tears of anger filled her eyes; I don't think I'd ever seen her so mad. I almost had to wrestle her to the ground to keep her from driving out to the guy's house and challenging him to a fight. It made a queer kind of sense, though; she'd been so frustrated with me for so many months, and had struggled to keep her temper under control all that time, but now that I had again done something she was proud of she wasn't about to let some pedant ruin it.

I managed to convince my mother that my feelings weren't hurt and that the man's review hadn't crushed me; in fact, reading his comments had brought a familiar sensation back to me. It was the same feeling I'd had whenever Sensei O'Keefe yelled at me, the feeling that I must have found a true master at last. If this guy thinks my playing is so bad, I thought, maybe he's the teacher I need. I called him the next day and made an appointment for a lesson.

When I showed up for my first lesson Mr. Turner set me up in a music room, sat back in a black leather chair and said, "All right, I'm not sure I remember what your playing was like. Play whatever you want." He looked like the lawyer Alan Dershowitz, and had not smiled once since I arrived.

The only piece of Western music I knew was the Bach, so I started in on it. After five bars he was wincing; he wasn't putting it on, either—he was actually in pain.

"OK, OK," he said, stopping me. "I remember now. You don't have to go on."

Mr. Turner sat quietly for a moment, as if not sure where to begin. "I have to tell you that I think that was the worst cello playing I've ever heard in a competition," he said. He seemed to be waiting to see if I would get angry and leave. When I didn't budge he got up, picked up his own cello and said, "Listen for a minute, and watch me closely."

He glanced at my copy of the music, frowned, then tossed it on the ground like a pair of filthy underwear. "The first thing I want you to do is to go home and burn that edition," he said. Then he closed his eyes and played the piece from memory.

He was great; I hadn't heard cello playing like that up close since the Parisot concert when I was seven. His body was completely relaxed, as if it took no effort at all for him to play like that.

When he finished Mr. Turner looked at me and said, "Who are you studying with now?"

"No one. I haven't had a lesson since I was thirteen."

"Oh! no wonder!" he shouted. "Why didn't you say so? OK, so maybe you're not the *worst* cellist I've ever heard! But wait a minute—who sponsored you for the competition?"

I told him the whole story of how I'd done it so that my parents wouldn't think I had ruined my life.

"Ah, ah. I see. OK. Maybe it's not all that bad after all. If you'd been studying with someone, that would have been bad news because by now you shouldn't be having all those technical problems. Maybe we can solve them; there's hope now. But what is it you want out of this? What's your goal?"

I really hadn't given this much thought. I was already starting to get bored with jazz; what was I going to do? It was one of those odd situations where you feel obliged to come up with a life plan in an instant, so I did my best: "I'll be going to Yale in the fall, and I want to major in music. Ultimately I'd like to perform."

"Not as a cellist?" he asked, looking doubtful.

"Yes. If I work hard starting now, could I get in shape in time?"

He shook his head, finally smiling. "You know who teaches at Yale, don't you? Aldo Parisot! I'll be perfectly honest with you. If he heard you play right now he'd sue for damages. I really don't know if you're being realistic here. . . . I mean, there's nothing wrong with being a good amateur."

Amateur! How I hated that word! "What if I work *really, really* hard?" I asked.

"Mm . . ."

"I mean *really* hard," I repeated, unintentionally gesturing with my hand the way Mr. Rowland had always done.

He shrugged. "I guess you've got to try. But listen, if it doesn't work out, I don't want you saying that I led you on or anything. I'll be straight with you. Every single cellist I know who plans to major in cello at college and go on to a performance career is several long years ahead of you in terms of technique. I'm not saying it's impossible, exactly, but you should be aware that it would be highly unusual if you pulled it off." He paused. "*Highly* unusual. Just so you know."

If I had been a true pessimist like my dad, I would have taken the man's cautionary advice to heart. But being a synthetic pessimist, I reacted in precisely the opposite way. His grim prognosis filled me with so much energy that I could barely sit still through the lesson; the thought that proving him wrong and beating the odds would redeem me, wash away my sins and make me a genuine hero made me feel alive in a way I hadn't felt since getting my white belt from Sensei O'Keefe. Kung fu had been silly, though; this was a serious calling, and this time I was fighting to climb back from a genuine fall. It was uphill this time, my back was against the wall, the chips were down, a lot was at stake, and my reputation—my whole life, actually—depended on it. I got busy starting that very night.

16

My fears that The Incident had ruined my relationship with my parents forever proved exaggerated. As soon as I started getting up early in the morning again, my father relaxed, and as long as I practiced Bach every night my mother seemed convinced that I would turn out fine. After ten weeks on the job I'd saved over a thousand dollars, and this time it was going straight into the bank. No more throwing money away on cars, I decided. My dad had just bought my mother a used Karmann Ghia, so now I could pick Annette up in something sportier than a bus and didn't feel the same need to have my own car.

Halfway through my eleventh week at work I nullified my wise, money-saving decision by demolishing the Karmann Ghia. I was on my way to see Annette right after dinner one night, I had a green light at a familiar intersection, I was driving within the speed limit, I had signaled my left turn, and I had been straight for two months, but it was dusk and for some reason I didn't see the full-size American car coming from the opposite direction. We crashed head-on, and the Karmann Ghia got the worst of it by far. I wasn't wearing a seat belt and my face went right into the pre-safety-glass windshield, but I was saved from serious injury by a stupid hat that I had made myself out of a piece of leather Scott had given me. Inspired by something I'd seen on a poster for the movie *Shaft*, I had designed it and sewn it together by hand. It looked OK from a distance, but I could never keep it on my head; I had failed to put any sort of elastic band or stiff frame in it, so I had to flop it over the top of my head and let it lie there like a beanbag pillow that had lost most of its beans. I couldn't wear it outdoors because the normal movement of walking or the slightest breeze made it slide off my head, so I kept it in the car and wore it when I drove. When our cars crashed, it slid down over my face and acted as a shield, so all I got was a bruise on my forehead. Fortunately the other fellow wasn't hurt at all, and when he saw me climb out of the wreck unscathed, he was too relieved to even be angry. I was very lucky.

I climbed out and looked at what had once been our sporty Volkswagen. "My dad is going to be real mad about this," I remember telling the other man, and I started trying to unbend the metal with my hands for some reason that seemed plausible at the time. As a policeman filled out a report, my eighth-grade earth science teacher drove by, stopped to see if anybody needed CPR (he taught the course every year, but never got to use it in real life), then offered to drive me home. "My dad is going to be real mad about this," I kept saying, but the earth science teacher insisted that my parents would both be glad I was alive.

The Karmann Ghia was towed away, the flares burned out, the policeman gave me a ticket and then it was time to go home. After reassuring me that my dad probably would not kill me, my former teacher dropped me off and I made the long walk up the driveway. When I went into the house my mother said, "Mark, you're all pale! Are you all right?"

"I totaled the car. Nobody was hurt. I'll pay for it, though—I have over a thousand dollars in the bank."

"You're sure you're OK? Nobody was hurt?" Dad asked.

"Yeah. It's just the car."

Dad closed his eyes and exhaled. Other dads threw fits when their kids crashed cars, but mine closed his eyes and sighed. In my mind, I had it worse than those other kids; when he sighed it meant that things were going just as he'd always thought they would, and nothing seemed quite so awful as feeling responsible for helping make things turn out the way he expected them to.

I went straight down to the basement and began practicing the mantra that I would be reciting constantly for the next ten days and nights:

Why didn't I see that car?

Let's replay that again. Crash! Shit.

Why didn't I stay home to watch those last five minutes of I Love Lucy?

Why didn't I see that car?

It took ten weeks for the car to be fixed, and during that time, since Mom had no car, Dad and I had to do all the grocery shopping on our way home from Greenwich. It was a depressing task; it was still winter, it was pitch-black out on our ride home, Dad was always exhausted, I was always starving, and the last thing either of us wanted to do was push a shopping cart across a dark, slush-covered parking lot and then wander through a glaringly bright supermarket to pick up fish sticks, TV dinners and spaghetti sauce. It was all my fault, but Dad never once gave in to the temptation of saying, "Look what I have to go through because of you!" which almost made it worse, because then I felt obliged to think it for him over and over, incorporating it into my regular mantra.

"Cheer up, fresh-face, these are the best years of your life," Ed made the mistake of saying to me one afternoon when I was sitting in the corner of the mail room looking at the accident report form I had to send to the Department of Motor Vehicles. I could stand being called fresh-face, I could put up with doing half of his job for him, but nobody was going to get away with telling me that being seventeen was something I ought to be happy about.

I whirled around and said through clenched teeth, "Ed, if these are the best years of my life, then would you do me a favor? Instead of giving me rubbers, would you mind picking up a gun and a box of bullets for me? Actually, just one bullet would be fine."

He looked confused. "What, you wanna kill me just for saying that? Some sense of humor."

Jesus. The guy couldn't get anything right. I picked up an envelope that had to be hand-delivered and stalked out of the building. I was in one of those moods where you are so frustrated, so angry, and yet so helpless that you forget where you are for long stretches of time, carrying on imaginary conversations in which you try so hard to defend or explain yourself that you even start talking out loud without realizing it. I was doing exactly that when I heard a quiet, firm voice say, "That's a poor walk, young man."

I stopped in my tracks. Was it in my head or did somebody actually talk to me? I turned around and saw an extremely old man wearing a black felt hat, a full-length black wool coat and black shoes polished to a mirror finish. He was standing in front of the library as if waiting for someone to pick him up. He stood ramrod-straight and had his gaze fixed directly in front of him.

"Did you say something to me?" I asked.

He turned his head and looked me straight in the eye. "I did. I said, 'That's a poor walk, young man.' "

He seemed to expect me to shrug and walk off. But there was something eerily sane about him, and this intrigued me.

"What do you mean?" I asked.

"What I mean is, you are walking on the balls of your feet and bouncing. It's not attractive; it's not the way a man should walk. A man should walk deliberately, first on the heels, then onto the balls of the feet, keeping his back straight, head erect, and moving smoothly."

For a second I felt of wave of annoyance pass through me. Old coot, I ought to ask him if he still remembers what it was like to walk on the balls of his feet. Then I thought, Maybe he's senile. This made me feel sorry for him. But then I looked at him again and saw that clearly he wasn't saying it to annoy me, and he didn't seem particularly concerned whether I took him seriously or not. Eerie.

"Can you show me what you mean?" I asked him.

"Yes." He demonstrated, first by imitating me, then by walking properly. This fellow had real presence.

Oh, what the hell. I walked in front of him a few times, trying to imitate his proper walk, until he was satisfied. Then I said, "Can I ask you why you would bother to tell me this, though?"

"Because you might not realize it if someone didn't tell you. A man looks more like a man if he holds himself confidently, moves smoothly and acts deliberately. And you'll find that if you hold yourself that way, you'll begin to act that way."

I must not have looked convinced because finally he grinned and added, "I taught at West Point for over thirty years. There's my daughter now. Good luck, son. Stay off the balls of your feet."

He got into a Mercedes with tinted windows and disappeared. I can't say that his advice stuck with me for long, but the encounter did lift my spirits for the rest of that day. When I told my dad about it on our drive home that evening, he seemed pleased with me.

"I'm glad you didn't brush him off," he said. "I'll bet you made that guy's day. He probably had people snapping to attention and hanging on his every word for most of his life, then one day, poof—Here's your gold watch, pal, go home and watch TV. And just like that, suddenly the world treats him differently. He's not a soldier anymore, he's just another old man who takes forever at the checkout line. Damn, I look forward to retiring, but I sure as hell don't look forward to becoming a useless old man. That was nice of you to listen to him like that."

It's funny how when you're a teenager and you're in the doghouse with your parents, you can't imagine how you'll ever get out of it. You try to picture the sorts of things you could do to win favor with them again, but they'd have to be heroic deeds, superhuman feats—things that even Mother Teresa would have to struggle to accomplish. But then one day you do some simple, tiny thing without even thinking about it and all of a sudden you're out of the doghouse. Parents are strange.

The car got fixed, I started putting money in the bank again, and my Bach slowly improved. The Winter of Guilt ended at last. Spring and summer passed without any further Incidents, and Mr. Turner warmed up to me slowly. By August I thought my playing had improved dramatically, so I asked him if he thought I had a shot at a career now.

"Well," he said, "you have gotten better, but let's face it, there's a lot of people out there who are still a lot better than you are. But whether or not you can make a career out of it isn't everything, Mark. The main thing is, you can get pleasure from it for the rest of your life."

Pleasure? I thought. Who said anything about *pleasure?* If I wanted pleasure, I would have done something *fun,* for God's sake, not play the cello. I should have realized right then that something was wrong, but I didn't. I honestly believed I could tough it out and become a soloist through sheer determination.

Right around the end of August I decided to treat myself to a little present for having made it to college without a criminal record: I went to hear the cellist Yo-Yo Ma in concert. As he came out onstage and the audience erupted into applause I thought, "Enjoy it now, buddy, because in five years I'm gonna give you a run for your money." Then he started playing.

Five minutes into his first piece my heart was already broken, and I left at intermission. I'd heard and seen enough. I vowed not to breathe a word of what had happened to my parents, though; I'd deal with it once I got to New Haven.

What had happened was that, first of all, his technique was so indescribably flawless that I knew in an instant that I could never, not even in two lifetimes, come close to it. Second, his musicality and musical instincts were so original, so genuine and so many-layered that it revealed most of my musicality to be a clever imitation at best. But the worst part by far was seeing him up there smiling. He was enjoying himself! He loved that music, he loved every phrase of it, and that was the real gulf between him and me.

The moment Yo Yo Ma began playing I began to see in my mind, like a collage of documentary film clips, the story of my interest in the cello. Beginning with wanting to please my parents, continuing with wanting to please my parents, taking a brief detour into jazz to prove that I was my own man, finding out that being my own man made my parents annoyed with me, then wrapping up with—guess what—wanting to please my parents! It was not that I thought wanting to please my parents was nec- essarily a bad thing; it was that I realized it wasn't a sound foundation for a career in classical music. When I looked at a sheet of music, I saw a bunch of symbols that indi- cated what to do with my fingers and arms when I held a box of wood with strings on it. I was musical enough to know when I was playing the notes wrong, but once they were in tune and in time I figured my job was over, I'd done my bit. When do I get to do this in front of people? For me music was a means of acquiring an identity. I as- sumed that if I worked hard, put in enough time and ef- fort, it would be like studying for a contractor's license; eventually I'd pass the test, be allowed to work and make money, and people would have to take me seriously. It honestly had not occurred to me to worry that I never was turned on by the music itself.

I tried to remember if, in all of my record collection, I had a single classical record. I didn't. I had never once taken the initiative to listen to one of my mother's records, either, and between hearing Aldo Parisot play when I was seven and hearing Yo Yo Ma play when I was seventeen, had never gone to any concerts but my mother's. The conclusion was inescapable: I didn't like classical music very much.

God, how it hurt to think this. In particular I felt like a traitor to my mother. This admission also left me suddenly without a clue about what to do with the rest of my life. Worst of all, it made me feel like a jackass. Why had it taken me until now to figure out something as obvious as the necessity of enjoying music if you planned to make a living at it? I didn't say anything about it to anyone, least of all to my parents. I went to my last cello lesson, thanked Mr. Turner for all his help, and as I drove home that night thought over and over, This is really a bad situation.

On my last day at work the secretaries treated me to a big lunch, and then threw a surprise party for me at the end of the day. Toasts were made, speeches were given, gifts were presented. When I left the office I had to use one of the canvas mail sacks to carry all my packages to the car. I got in—Dad was on vacation, so I was by myself—pulled out of the parking lot and felt guilty the whole drive home. I felt guilty because I believed that in just one week I was going to go to Yale, announce that I was no longer interested in music, and be sent home in disgrace because I had been accepted as a music major. Then I would have to go right back to the law firm, explain what had happened, and at least make the gesture of offering to give everyone's presents back. I kept them all in their packages and made sure the name tags were still attached so I wouldn't embarrass myself later.

The day came. Mom, Dad, Erich, Rachel, Annette and I piled into the old bus for the drive to New Haven. When we got there we couldn't find a parking space anywhere near campus ("I hate this shithole of a city," Dad kept muttering), so we had lunch together in the downtown New Haven McDonald's. Not wanting to make them drive back into all that traffic, I pulled my suitcase of clothes and my cello out of the car and said my good-byes in front of McDonald's. The car started to drive away, then stopped and backed up. My dad stuck his head out the window and said, "Don't come home until you've made something of yourself."

"He's only kidding, honey, he's only kidding!" That was Mom, living proof that irony is not contagious.

I walked to the campus and found my room. My roommate hadn't arrived yet, so I spent the rest of the day and the night alone in the empty dorm. I had trouble getting to sleep; for some reason I could only think of all the things I had done that I regretted: how we are given only one childhood, how I had had seventeen years to make mine a good one but instead had turned it into something like a Cheech and Chong movie. Of course at some level I understood that nobody is perfect, that everybody must leave home sometime, and that my parents would certainly not prefer that I stay in their basement and work in the mail room for the rest of my life. But that mature understanding was seriously challenged by my immature sense of overall shame, an emotion that had grown strong with use, particularly in the past year. At ten o'clock I started sniffling, by ten-thirty I was sobbing, and from eleven on I was just plain bawling.

At two in the morning a deafening roar from the street below interrupted my tearful meditations. I peered down out of my window and saw a whole pack of Hell's Angels on their choppers sitting at the intersection waiting for the light to turn green. It took a moment to take it all in—a whole tribe of scowling rebels with leather outfits, studs all over the place, Nazi helmets, cobra tattoos, metal-tipped boots, throbbing, screaming, chrome-covered bombs between their legs, biker babes clinging to their backs, sitting at a completely empty intersection at two in the morning waiting obediently for the traffic light to change. I stopped crying and started laughing instead. Maybe I *had* made a fool of myself as a kid, and maybe I *was* lost without a compass now, but looking at those guys made me feel better. Maybe my dad was right to believe that we are all pathetically deceived about who we really are and why we really do what we do. It depressed my father to think this way, but on that first night at college the thought that all human beings might be pathetic came as a great relief to me because it got me off the hook. After the light turned green and the Hell's Angels roared off to their next appointment with danger and anarchy, I wrote my folks a letter thanking them for all they had done on my behalf; I figured that even if I did get sent home soon, they would have some document showing that they had done a good job to get me this far. Once I had done this, I was able to fall asleep.

My roommate showed up the next day. His name was Holden Young. He was Chinese American, tall, athletic, beautifully dressed, supernaturally handsome, had gone to a high-powered prep school, and was a soccer and tennis star. Apparently in its wisdom the student housing department thought we might have something in common—namely, China. But Holden, an all-American dreamboat who had already aced calculus, organic chemistry and Latin in high school, didn't seem to know much about China, whereas I, the yokel from Ridgefield who had tried to grow pot in his parents' house, had never seen a soccer game or a tennis match, so it took some time for us to figure each other out. The first thing he did upon arriving was to tack up a poster of a soccer ball bulging through the net after having streaked past the goalie. It was one of those slightly three-dimensional posters made of thin plastic, so the ball really did stick out a bit. Over my bed I had hung one of my paintings of a guy in a robe with a topknot staring at a waterfall.

"You play any sports?" Holden asked.

"No, but I did kung fu for a few years." Holden looked suspicious. Another white kid who took kung fu lessons; I think he was afraid I was going to ask if his family kept ancestral tablets in their living room.

"Do you speak Chinese?" I asked him.

"Only the words for sweet and sour pork," he answered, and I'm sure that in turn I must have looked disappointed. But within an hour we discovered that in fact we did have something in common: we both couldn't wait to look at the pictures of our female classmates in the freshman directory.

For me it was a bit of a theoretical exercise because I was still going out with Annette and only twenty-four hours earlier had pledged eternal fidelity. But for Holden, who was unattached, it was a very real concern, and I enjoyed helping him with his research. Part of my enjoyment, I'm sure, can be explained by analogy: helping Holden find a girlfriend was something like how I imagined it would be to help Neil Armstrong get a job as a commercial pilot—you could brainstorm freely, knowing that your man's qualifications were beyond dispute.

We went to all of the orientations together, played Frisbee together out on the lawn (he could throw it with either hand, flick it like a bottle cap, catch it on his raised elbow or pop it up with his heel and make it land on his head like a hat) and accompanied each other to the mixers at night. Those were the days before the nationwide crackdown on students' consumption of alcohol, so you didn't have to walk more than a hundred yards before reaching a table set up with free beer, wine, mixed drinks or hard liquor—all served in giant plastic pails. Expensive, powerful stereo systems propped in windows all over campus competed with one another for supremacy, treating us to a never-ending auditory menu of Van Halen, Hendrix, Aerosmith, Lynyrd Skynyrd, Pink Floyd, Kiss and Fleetwood Mac. I was beginning to like college, which made it all the worse, because I assumed I was going to get kicked out for quitting the cello.

On the fifth day I had to face reality. I had an eleven o'clock appointment with my assigned faculty adviser to discuss my course schedule. His office, I noted grimly, was in the new School of Music building. The moment of truth had arrived.

Apparently the building had just been completed; it looked brand-new and masking tape was still on some of the windows. As I walked down the echoing hallway toward my adviser's office, I passed by several practice rooms, all of them occupied by serious-looking young virtuosi. To my relief, I noted that at least one segment of the student body appeared more out of it than me. All the males in the practice rooms had frightful cowlicks and at least one sneaker untied, while the females all seemed to be wearing pillowcases with holes cut out for their arms and heads.

I entered the professor's office at the appointed time and he offered me a seat. In contrast to the students in the practice rooms, he was rather dashing; he had silver hair that flowed down almost to his shoulders, a neat silver mustache and a kindly, wise, European-looking face. It was the kind of face you couldn't lie to, and I didn't see any point in dragging things out.

"Sir, I don't know exactly how to explain this, but I've decided that I'm not cut out to be a cellist."

"Really?"

"Yes. Even the thought of practicing now makes me—"

"Sick to your stomach?"

"Yeah . . ."

His face broke into a grin. "I think that's marvelous!" he said cheerily. "What other interests might you have?"

I was confused. "But, sir, I applied as a music major. Doesn't that mean that I have to . . . I don't know . . . reapply to one of the other schools and wait till next year?"

He paused for a beat, then laughed jovially. "Is that why you look so glum? Son, you don't have to reapply or explain this to anyone! It doesn't matter at all what you *said* you wanted to major in when you applied. Once you're accepted as an undergraduate, you can major in anything you like. When I said that it was marvelous, what I meant was that it's good that you've realized this now, as opposed to two or three years from now, when it would be too late to switch majors and you would have to stick it out just to graduate. Do you have any idea how often that happens, particularly with music? So many kids get pushed into music when they're young, they do it for all the wrong reasons, then they get to college and keep at it out of a sense of guilt and they hate it. What a waste! There's no point to music if you don't love it."

Wow. This guy was amazing. "Are you a musician, sir?"

"Who, me? No, I'm a photographer. They just stuck me in this building because it's the only one where I could fit my darkroom."

A long-haired photographer was my faculty adviser. Wow. I was *really* starting to like this school.

"So to go back to my earlier question, Mr. Salzman, do you have any other interests at the moment?"

I couldn't think of a thing.

"Well, then, you should find a nice place on campus to sit, take a good look through the course book and see if anything appeals to you. Visit a few classes, listen to a few lectures. You have a couple of weeks to decide, you know. When you have some ideas, give me a call and we'll make sure you're covering the distribution requirements and so on. Enjoy yourself; there's too much here to not find something that turns you on!"

Drunk with relief, I stumbled down the hallway and out the main entrance. Taped to one of the window panels of the main door, I saw a piece of paper with a handwritten note announcing, "Welcome to your new practice building! Take good care of it!" I laughed out loud. I'd take good care of it, all right; when I graduated someday, I would probably be the only prospective music major who could honestly say that he had left the building in exactly the same condition that he had found it.

By the time I had finished reading the course book, I almost wished I *had* been kicked out. It was the most intimidating document I had ever seen. I asked Holden to help me figure out what classes to visit, and he showed me the schedule he had worked out for himself. He had a biology class, a chemistry class, an English class, a physics class, a U.S. history class and a French class. Using his schedule as a model, I worked out a similar menu of courses. The next day I visited a biology class, a math class and a chemistry class. All of them were listed as introductory. When I got to the lecture halls I picked up copies of the syllabi, and that was when my agony really began. I couldn't even understand the course descriptions! The lectures were so far over my head that I left each of the classes after ten minutes. Defeated, I went back to my room and told Holden I wasn't cut out for college.

"Did you go to any of the Chinese classes?" he asked. "I mean, that's something you already know about. Why not give that a try?"

I had briefly thought of that, but whenever I tried to think of studying Chinese again I got a stomachache thinking of my earlier foolishness: all those kung fu lessons, eating with chopsticks, walking to school barefoot, the incense—it was too embarrassing to face all over again. But Holden had a point; at least it was a subject I had some chance of being qualified to pursue. Holden found the listing in the course book, but then winced and said, "Oh, no, you're not going to want to do this."

"Why not?"

He pointed to the course listing. "That building's in the middle of nowhere," he said, "at least a half-hour walk from here. And look, first-year Chinese meets from eight-thirty to ten-thirty in the morning! Forget it! Let's find you something else."

I explained to Holden that out of sheer habit I was up by six every morning every day anyway, so the time wasn't a problem. "Oh," he said, stroking his chin thoughtfully. "Is that why you disappear before ten every night? It never occurred to me that you might actually be going to sleep."

The next morning I was at the East Asian languages building before eight and got the best chair in the classroom. Gradually other students trickled in, all of them looking bleary-eyed. At eight-twenty-five the instructor arrived, a tall, thin, fine-boned, elegant Chinese woman; she was probably in her sixties, but she moved like a thirty-year-old. All of the students, I noticed, came to life the instant she arrived and started beaming with pleasure. As soon as she began the class I knew why.

Mrs. Li was hands-down the most charismatic, comic, energetic and enthusiastic language instructor any of us had ever seen. Those first two hours were not so much a class as they were a case of interactive performance art. Introducing the phrase *kaiche* (to drive a car), she thrust out her arms, grasped an imaginary steering wheel, bent her knees 90 degrees so that her thighs were parallel to the ground, then shuffled between the desks, honking a horn and trying to parallel-park. She finished the demonstration by skidding and crashing into her desk, then shrugging and explaining in a loud stage whisper, "What can I say, dears? *Chinese driver!*"

The touch that made all of this so entertaining was the contrast between Mrs. Li's dignified appearance and her outlandish clowning; if you can imagine Grace Kelly teaching a beginning dance class by acting out Buster Keaton routines, you'll get the picture. The other thing was that she somehow managed to shower individual attention on every student. If you sneezed in class, Mrs. Li gave you a tissue, Sudafed tablets and a glass of water; if you coughed, she gave you cough drops and a scarf to wear home. If you did well on a test, Mrs. Li led a one-woman parade around the classroom in your honor; if you did poorly, she tutored you privately until you improved. Every student was smitten with her, and Mrs. Li's most impressive gift of all was the ability to make each of us think that we were really her favorite. I chose all the rest of my classes around this one.

From that day on I loved college. I loved the classes, I loved the homework, I loved the starchy food, and I loved introducing myself as Holden Young's roommate. "Really?" people would ask, their faces inevitably brightening. The boys would follow this with, "Holden Young? The soccer player? Cool," while the women would glance from side to side to make sure no one was eavesdropping on the conversation, then say, "He's the most gorgeous Asian guy on campus." My association with him became the foundation of my social life, which was fine with me. One might imagine that it would have been torturous for me, five foot seven, skinny, a Chinese-studies nerd and full-time secretary of the Mrs. Li Fan Club, to have to live with such a monumental stud, but what redeemed Holden entirely was that he was not a playboy at all; he was even more shy around women than I was. He would stare at the freshman directory with one hand on the telephone and stay frozen that way until it came time either to eat, sleep or go to class. He ended up having one relationship during his whole college career, whereas I had two. By my calculations that makes me twice as virile as Holden Young, a statistic that gives me pleasure to this day.

17

My freshman year of college brought me the longest uninterrupted stretch of happiness that I'd known since the year my parents brought home our first used color-television set. My mind was almost constantly occupied, so time lost its usual meaning. I no longer measured time in hours, as I had at work, or in minutes, as I had while practicing the cello, or in seconds, as I had during algebra class or school dances. Now I seemed aware only of days and weeks. Every teacher I had was clearly passionate about his or her subject, and they gave the impression during their lectures of stretching their own minds to their limits, which I found highly contagious. Most of the students at Yale were passionate about something as well, although not necessarily academics. Many of them took their interests to the same extremes that I had, if not further. One fellow, known as the Morse Monocle Man because he lived in Morse residential college, was so interested in turn-of-the-century European history that he wore period clothes, a period haircut, refused to go out in bright sunlight without a period hat and wore a monocle even when he showered. The first time I saw him was in Sterling Library hunched over a book; I thought he was a wax-museum figure set up as part of an Oscar Wilde exhibit. At the other end of the spectrum was a woman whose legal name was Bird of the Phoenix Movement; I'm not sure what her interests were, but she wore ponchos, beads and floppy hats, and dyed the fur of her enormously popular dog (nontoxic edible dye, I'm sure) a different color every month. For the first time in my life I was a comparatively normal member of a community; I could have worn my baldhead wig if I'd wanted to.

Most of all, though, I loved the work. It was like preparing for the Ch'ing Game all over again, only this time *all* of my professors were as enthusiastic as Mr. Rowland, all of them stayed long enough to finish their courses, and I got to play the Game at the end, which at Yale was to write a long paper with lots of footnotes, and to take the final exam in a historic auditorium. And this time everybody around me was preparing for the Game, too. I felt like Steve Martin in *The Jerk* when he finally bids farewell to his adoptive black family, moves into a white community, and discovers that he's not alone after all, that there is a whole world of people out there who crave Twinkies and tap their feet to Lawrence Welk tunes just as he does. Yale was a nerd's paradise.

Once I had become an aspiring China scholar again, it was only a matter of time before I got the urge to dust off my kung fu uniform and throw a few dragon punches and tiger-tail kicks. By spring I was practicing on and off again in the steam tunnels under the dormitory. Holden came back to the room from soccer practice one day with a flyer advertising a martial arts competition that weekend—the Yale Open—and suggested I try competing. I had nothing to lose, so on the day of the competition I showed up and began filling out the form. Then I realized I had to choose a rank for myself. Sensei had always insisted that his ranks bore no resemblance to the ranks any other schools in Connecticut were giving, so I wasn't sure where I stood. If I chose too low a rank it would look bad; everybody hates it at karate competitions when someone who should be a brown belt competes as a yellow belt just to get a trophy. I looked at the categories: white belt, yellow belt, green belt, brown belt, black belt. Oh, what the hell, I thought, and checked the box next to black belt.

From a certain point of view, I could feel proud of the result: I took first place in forms and second place in fighting. From another point of view, however, it was a limited success, as there were only two competitors in the black-belt division. My opponent was a young assistant professor who was very serious about karate, however, so it was not a completely meaningless exercise, and our sparring bout in the finals, which was also our elimination bout, was exciting. If only Sensei O'Keefe were here to see this, I thought as the chief judge hung the medals around my neck—but then I changed my mind when I remembered that he would have beaten me within an inch of my life for the unforgivable sin of awarding myself a black belt without first having dealt with Auggie Doggie or Doggie Daddy.

My experience at the tournament inspired me to start practicing every day, but a few weeks later an event occurred that forced me to rethink my commitment to martial arts yet again. For several days I had been exchanging glances with a young woman who usually studied just across a long wooden table from me in the library. (Annette and I had broken up just after Christmas. When you're seventeen and have no car, a separation of fifty miles makes it a long-distance-relationship, and I failed the long-distance-relationship test.) The woman in the library and I gradually started saying hello to each other, then making small talk, and one afternoon she surprised me by asking if I wanted to take a break and have a walk around the library with her.

We strolled around the campus, which was particularly beautiful, as the young leaves were finally appearing on the trees and the spring flowers were in full bloom. From where we walked we could see a row of blossoming trees in the old cemetery near the library, and she suggested that we have a closer look.

In the cemetery we paused to sit on an unmarked sarcophagus and were in the middle of a conversation about what papers we had to write when a young black man wearing a leather trench coat appeared from behind a tree and approached us. Something about the way he walked toward us looked wrong. Then I remembered a bit of advice that a representative of the campus police had given us at one of the orientation ceremonies: Never hang out in the cemetery. When the man got close he said, "Hey, any of you got a match?"

"No, sorry."

Then he opened the trench coat to reveal a lead pipe in his right hand.

"Gimme all your money or I'll split both your heads open," he ordered, waving the lead pipe close to his leg.

The way he was standing with it, all I had to do was

228

rush him and hit him hard once in the face and he would have been done for. A kick to the balls would have worked. Hell, the woman I was with could have pushed him and he would have stumbled backward, fallen over a gravestone and been knocked out. But that's not what happened.

What happened was that I was so shocked, so utterly terrified, so transported beyond any level of fear that I had ever known before, that I hallucinated. Everything suddenly became perfectly calm, perfectly quiet and perfectly all right. I felt happy! He didn't seem like such a bad guy. I handed him my wallet without any feeling of anger or resentment at all. When the woman I was with extended her purse toward him, the man said, "No, not you. Just him." He was a gentleman! I liked him more and more.

"You got anything else?" he asked me.

I remembered that one of the secretaries in Greenwich had given me a watch as a farewell present but that I didn't like the feel of it on my wrist, so I always carried it in my pocket. Of course!

"Yes!" I answered cheerfully, and handed it over. Then he said, "I'll be watching you," backed away from us, turned and disappeared among the gravestones. I was smiling; I thought it was a rather nice encounter. The woman I was with grabbed onto my arm and held it tightly. When I turned to face her, she let go of my arm and hugged me hard, chest to chest. Wherever you are, I thought to the man with the lead pipe, thank you.

About halfway back to the library, however, I started to come back to reality. My hands started to shake, my legs felt weak, and then it occurred to me what a total, hands-down, pathetic, world-class coward I was. Not only did I not prevent that criminal from getting away with robbery and threatened assault, not only did I not avoid becoming a victim, not only did I not take advantage of the man's ridiculously vulnerable posture, but *I didn't even think of martial arts* until ten minutes after it had happened. Being reasonable, as most women are when it comes to matters of violence, my companion was relieved that neither of us had gotten hurt, and she reassured me that she was glad I had not tried anything foolish or heroic.

But I was deeply troubled. I don't mean just upset; I mean that for the next solid two weeks I couldn't concentrate on anything long enough to read or write a sentence, much less work on my final papers. All I could think of was that Sensei O'Keefe had been right all along. Sure, he was an asshole, but he was right: I was a pathological sissy. I saw that man with the lead pipe standing in front of me all day long. I relived the encounter thousands of times. Down in the steam tunnels I demolished him, I destroyed him, I maimed him, I bit him, I crippled him, I disemboweled him, I tore his eyes out, I knocked every one of his teeth out and made a necklace with them, and I delivered impassioned speeches over his dead body, with the president of Yale and the mayor of New Haven standing behind me waiting to give me the Town/Gown Joint Medal of Honor. But each one of these imagined victories faded, and I was left with the sickening memory of how completely vulnerable I had been. If he had said, "Kneel down now so I can split your head open," I probably would have done it without realizing what I was doing. My only consolation—and it was precious little—was that at least my dad's prediction about how I would cope with danger hadn't come entirely true: I hadn't shit my pants.

My excruciating shame let up just enough for me to finish my work for the semester. Of course I stopped practicing kung fu in the steam tunnels; what a waste of time that had turned out to be. One morning I noticed a poster for the Yale Karate Club taped to the bulletin board of the East Asian languages building. It showed a cartoon of a tough-looking bulldog wearing a karate suit, below which a line boasted, "Walk in confidence!" Walk in confidence, my ass. Breaking the taboo against defacing property, I took a Magic Marker and altered it to read, "Walk in *false* confidence."

When the semester ended I went home and returned to my job in Greenwich. It wasn't the same, though; once I had gotten hooked on the pressure and rewards of academic life, I found it hard to go back to sorting mail with the same Zen-like enthusiasm. Also there wasn't anything for me to do at night, since I wasn't seeing Annette or playing the cello, and all of my other friends had moved away. It was even harder to talk with my dad than it had been before. I had the impression that once I had made it safely to college, he felt that the bulk of his mission as my father had more or less been completed and there wasn't much left for him to do. He seemed not to want to be a burden to me, which was hardly how I saw it. It was a long, dull summer, and I counted the days until I could go back to New Haven.

The fall semester of sophomore year was somehow even more enjoyable than my freshman year had been. The more advanced the courses got and the heavier the workload, the more turned on I got. Also, the more deeply I got into studying Chinese, the more tempted I became to have another look at Chinese philosophy. Maybe, I thought, if I could read it in the original language, it might make more sense. Whenever I discussed this with anyone in the Chinese department, they inevitably said the same thing: You need to talk to Tungli Shen. He was a poet and Chinese teacher at Yale, born in Canton and raised in Peking, who had learned most of the classical Chinese literary canon from his father, a graduate of the imperial examinations. Tungli Shen didn't just *know* Chinese literature, everyone told me; he could recite it from memory. They weren't kidding; scholars from all branches of Chinese studies came to him with literary queries, and the Smithsonian Institution, recognizing Mr. Shen as one of the few people alive who could recite T'ang poetry in the form of ancient chants, flew him to Washington to do a series of recordings for them. Everyone agreed that he was the living embodiment of the Chinese scholar/artist/philosopher ideal. But I didn't go to see him right away; I wanted to wait until I was better prepared.

In October I received an envelope in the mail with no return address. Inside was a newspaper clipping from my hometown paper announcing that Michael Dempsey had been promoted to black belt by Sensei Timothy P. O'Keefe. Accompanying the article was a photo of Michael flying through the air, planting his foot on his brother Frank's throat. He looked great.

He'd done it! He'd stuck it out for the long haul, and now he wore the black belt, just as Sensei had predicted. In fact, Michael was the only one of us from that 1974 group to get his black belt, also as Sensei had predicted. I felt proud of him. Even though martial arts hadn't worked out for me, I smiled inside thinking that someday some asshole might try to rob Michael in a cemetery, and, hoo boy, what a surprise that fellow would get. Several times I thought of calling him, but I didn't. I did fold up the article and keep it in my wallet, however.

During Christmas break I was home in Ridgefield when I got a call from Scott, my fellow State of Whoa traveler. There was going to be a big party on the other side of town and a lot of the old gang would be there. Did I want to come?

Did I want to come? I'd been watching *Gilligan's Island*, *Lost in Space* and *Star Trek* reruns all day, and had no other plans for that night except to watch *All in the Family* followed by *The Mary Tyler Moore Show*, followed by *The Bob Newhart Show*. I was there, man.

I drove over in the old VW bus. The poor Karmann Ghia, after getting repaired following my accident, had run well for a year and a half, but then my brother got his driver's license and had his turn at it. When *he* totaled it, it couldn't be fixed. Served him right, too, after spoiling my agricultural experiment the year before with that sneaky *World Book* ploy.

The party was in a big house that a group of guys from Western Connecticut State College were renting for the year. Scott and Lenny, the guy who drove the Triumph into the swamp, were there, and we had a good time reminiscing about our adventures, all of which seemed to have occurred many lifetimes ago. I mentioned that I'd heard that Michael had gotten his black belt.

"Oh, yeah," Scott said. Something about the way he said it made me curious.

"What? Have you seen him?"

"Sure. He's in the bathroom."

"Really?"

"Yep. He's getting kind of out of control."

"How so?"

"Oh, man, he's into some heavy shit lately."

"What? What did he do?"

"Oh, I don't know. Ask him yourself—you know him better than I do. I think he's headed for trouble soon. Go take a look at him."

Lenny laughed. "Don't be a fucking mom! Dempsey's cool, man. He'll be fine."

My curiosity was unbearable now. I went into the bathroom, but didn't see anyone. As I was leaving I heard a voice say, "Don't forget to close the door." It was Michael's voice, but where was he?

I pulled the shower curtain aside and there he was, lying on his back in the tub with all of his clothes on, covered with vomit.

"Barabbas!" he said warmly. He looked terrible—overweight, puffy-faced, pale and obviously exhausted. "How the fuck are you? I heard you're a nine-to-five chump now."

"Are you all right down there?"

"Fuck you! I could still kick *your* ass. I'm just . . . hanging out for a while, checking things out. Taking a break."

"Hey, congratulations on the black belt."

"Thanks. Did you hear about my test?"

"No. How was it?"

His eyes, already half closed throughout our conversation, closed all the way and he shook his head groggily. "Intense, man. You shoulda been there."

"If you'd told me about it, I'd have come to watch."

"No, you asshole! I mean you shoulda *been* there. You should never have cradded lessons, man. I'm gonna take a break now. Catch you later, Barabbas."

His head lolled around, then his chin rested on his chest

and he nodded off. When I returned to the party I said, "Shouldn't we be keeping an eye on him? He looks pretty bad."

"Aw, he'll be OK. He was speeding all day, so he took a downer to come down. He just needs some rest."

Back at school I was having a ball. I was too much of a nerd to worry that I spent most of my Friday and Saturday nights in the library, but part of the charm of Yale was that a whole network of adults had been hired by the university to worry about students' social life on their behalf. Early in the spring semester our residential college master threw a dinner party at her house on campus, and all members of the college were invited. But the invitation read "Jacket required." For most events like dances and mixers Holden happily lent me suitable clothes, even though they were all too big for me—he even taught me how to dance—and he would have been glad to outfit me this time, but when I mentioned the dinner party to my dad on the phone he said, "You don't have a real jacket, do you?"

"No."

"We have to get you one. It's about time you had at least one decent jacket, now that you're starting to go to parties like that."

That weekend Dad picked me up and took me home and we went shopping at a good used-clothes store my mother had heard about. They had only one jacket in my size, in dark gray corduroy, but it looked good on me and it was practically as good as new, so Dad got it for me. When we climbed back into the bus he looked at me and nodded, but he had a look on his face that demanded explanation.

"What?" I asked.

"Oh, I was just thinking."

"What?"

He paused, then finally said, "Nothing but the second-best for my son."

Wearing my new coat I attended the party, and after dinner we all moved to the living room, where we drank red wine and chatted by candlelight. As always at large social events with my peers, I felt nervous and was unable to initiate conversation with anyone. I was always fine once someone started talking to me, but I never did learn how to introduce myself to strangers. I found myself backing farther and farther away from the group, pretending to be interested in my cocktail napkin and wondering if it would be rude to leave early, not really watching where I was going. Suddenly I felt a hot stab in my back, right near my shoulder blade, and realized I had backed into someone's cigarette.

I was mortified, but my first thought was that if I moved suddenly, the person would realize that his or her cigarette had burned me. I didn't want to put anyone through that, so I slowly moved away from the source of the pain.

Instead of going away, though, the pain got worse. Much worse—and very fast. It was excruciating! Jesus, I thought, this guy must be following me on purpose with a cigar pressed into my coat. I was in agony. Then I noticed a woman pointing frantically at my shoulder. I glanced backward and saw that I was on fire. I had backed up against the piano where a candelabrum had been placed and had stood there like an ass until my beautiful brand-new secondhand jacket ignited. I tore off the flaming coat, threw it on the floor and kicked the fire out.

It was an embarrassing way to become the center of attention, and of course it was not the solution to my shyness that I was hoping for. I broke the tension by laughing it off, then excused myself and went home. There I told Holden what had happened and he asked me to turn around.

"Holy shit!" he said, trying not to laugh. "It didn't just burn through your coat! It burned through your sweater, your shirt and part of your skin! I think I can see your trapezius muscle. Or maybe that's the scapula? Wait—no, I think I see your spinal cord!"

"Shut up, Holden. Help me get these clothes off."

Holden gave me some iodine for the wound, and I turned in for the night. All I could think of was Why did it have to be my new jacket? Why did I have to back into a flame? Why didn't I jump away from the fire as soon as I felt it? Why was I such a *wuss*?

On a February afternoon I was reading an article about how it was taboo in Chinese villages for men or boys to walk under the drying laundry of women who were menstruating when the phone rang. It was my brother.

"Hey, Erich, what's up?"

"I have bad news. Michael Dempsey died this morning."

"Michael *died*?"

"Yeah, a car accident. He fell asleep at the wheel driving real late last night. Right near Ethan Allen Inn. You know that rocky slope? His car went off it. Lenny was in the car too but he's OK. The funeral's this weekend. You think you ought to come down for it?"

"Yeah, I better. I'll take the train to Westport. Can you pick me up?"

"I'll be at school, but Mom can pick you up. She figured you'd want to come back. Sorry to have to tell you such bad news."

As I rode the train home I didn't have much of an emotional reaction to the news. Part of me was taken by surprise; part of me thought it shouldn't have surprised anyone.

Still not feeling anything, I went to the wake the next day and had to face the awful sight of his mother, surrounded by her four other sons, weeping over his coffin. They had to keep it closed; it had been a bad accident. I said something to her about how sorry I was, then moved to the waiting room. Bill was there. "Hey," he said. He looked much smaller in a suit and tie.

"I heard it on the radio coming home from work," he said. "I couldn't believe it. At least he got his black belt, though. That was the one thing he wanted."

Michael's brother Frank came out to join us.

"Sorry, Frank," I said.

"Yeah, sorry about Mike, Frank."

Frank was in shock. "We buried him in his good uniform," he said slowly. "He would have wanted that."

When Mrs. Dempsey came out into the waiting room she looked a little better. She hugged me and I asked if there was anything I could do.

"Would you say something at the funeral tomorrow?" she asked. "Michael was always so proud of you, I know he'd like that."

"Sure."

I spent the rest of that day and night writing a eulogy. The next day, back at the funeral home before moving to the church, a commotion of whispers broke the silence. I turned to see the door open, and a man, barefoot and wearing a snow-white Oriental robe with his hair in a samurai-style topknot, walked slowly past all of us in our black, middle-class funeral outfits. He didn't look at anyone, he just walked steadily toward the coffin. What was shocking was that he wasn't Chinese or Japanese; it was Sensei O'Keefe.

All my young life I'd been told to tuck in my shirt and avoid wearing pants with holes in the knees at formal occasions because it wasn't "appropriate" to mess with the dress code. I had always thought that was just meaningless conformity until I saw Sensei in that white bedsheet at Michael's funeral. That was *really* inappropriate. He obviously meant it to be an expression of deep respect. I'm sure he'd made that robe himself, and the thought of that angry, tormented man spending hours hunched over it with a thread and needle, and then daring to wear it in that funeral parlor, was touching, but the effect was like a kick in the balls. He looked as if he had stopped by on his way to a Halloween party.

Sensei kneeled in front of the coffin Japanese style and meditated, then punched the coffin lightly, got up, returned to the back of the room and stood at attention. No one knew what to do or say.

The funeral director announced quietly that it was "time." Mrs. Dempsey moved toward the coffin, then fell backward in a faint. Sensei rushed forward and caught her in time, then bent over her, fanning her face and telling her to breathe deeply. When she recovered, Michael's brothers, the funeral director and I carried the coffin out to the hearse.

The service was in a Catholic church. Given that the priest wore a white robe, Sensei's outfit blended in slightly better than it had in the funeral home, but it was still all wrong. When the priest had nearly finished with the service, he walked over to me and said, "As you know, the family has asked that you say something. Are you going to be all right, son?"

I got the impression from the way he asked me that he was not keen on one of Michael's buddies giving a speech. I imagine he was worried I might get up and tell rock 'n' roll stories. "I'll be OK. It's short."

I got up and delivered my eulogy; then we moved to the cemetery and the coffin was lowered into the ground. It was freezing cold out, and wet snow covered the ground, but Sensei stood the whole time in bare feet and that flimsy sheet, not shivering once. After the ceremony was over, everyone left except for Sensei O'Keefe, who knelt in the snow beside the grave. As I drove out of the cemetery with my parents, I could see him still kneeling there.

"A lot of nerve that guy has," my mother said, her eyes red from crying, "to show up for a boy's funeral dressed like that. I wonder how that made poor Mrs. Dempsey feel."

"She has too much class to let it bother her, I'm sure," my dad said.

That night I went over to Michael's house, where dozens of relatives were hovering around Mrs. Dempsey, making sure there was plenty to eat and drink and that she didn't have to worry about anything.

One of the relatives, an aunt of Michael's, seemed especially stricken with grief. "Why does God take the best ones?" she kept asking. After dinner she took me aside and pointed to a boom box on the living-room table. "That was such a beautiful speech you gave," she said, sobbing quietly. "Would you please read it one more time for Michael's mother? I'd like to tape it for her. I know she'll treasure it."

She set up the box right there in the living room and hushed everyone up. I couldn't refuse, of course, but it was an awful thing to have to do. I read the speech again, and Mrs. Dempsey started crying with renewed vigor.

"Thank you," the aunt said, hugging me for a long time. Then she picked up the tape player. "Oh, sweet Mother of Jesus!" she said angrily. "How could I be so dumb? I pressed 'play' instead of 'record.' We'll have to do it once more."

18

The funeral was all about Michael, but once the ceremony was over, in my mind his death became all about me. I began examining my reactions to the event with dark fascination; I felt ashamed, though I wasn't sure why, that my strongest emotion that weekend had not been a sense of loss, but instead a sense of helplessness at not being able to comfort Michael's mother. I also felt vaguely guilty for having quit lessons and abandoning Michael when he probably most needed a close friend. But most disturbing of all was a growing sense that something was missing from my reaction to the event. I was sad, of course, but—and I felt extremely guilty for thinking this—wasn't there a larger component to this? Wasn't a person supposed to be shaken to the core by this sort of milestone, and forced to reevaluate his life?

This was, after all, someone exactly my age who, in one instant, and without having willed it, had gone from having his whole adult life in front of him to ceasing to exist forever. It was a momentous event, certainly the most serious one of my life, yet I felt unchanged. Awful as it is to admit, I felt almost disappointed. I was convinced that I had to make an effort to keep my mind on the experience until I had properly digested it; there had to be a message in this somewhere, one that was vital for me to understand if I was to move forward in my own life, but I couldn't decipher it. But if I didn't decipher it, it seemed to me, it would be from a lack of commitment to the ideal of leading an informed, examined life—and we all know what the unexamined life is worth. If I didn't decipher this message, I feared, I would regret it for the rest of my life.

Uncharacteristically for me, I did not discuss this with my father. I knew that he almost certainly would have his own interpretation, and would have been happy to pass it on to me. This sort of thing—the unexpected, the undeserved, the unbearable—was right up his alley. But I didn't want his interpretation, and I was sure he would understand why. I felt that the time had come for me to start answering these questions on my own.

When I returned to New Haven my friends and teachers offered me plenty of thoughtful attention, but rather than consoling me as it was supposed to, it only encouraged my sense of personal drama. Soon I felt I owed it to them as well as to Michael to draw some meaning out of the tragedy, so that his death, along with my friends' sincere concern, would not be for nothing.

It became difficult for me to concentrate on my schoolwork because any time that I spent reading Chinese or Victorian novels or articles about archaeological discoveries in Peru was time spent avoiding the far more relevant question: How do we move on? Why aren't we all paralyzed by the knowledge of our mortality? Ironically, the awareness of my own mortality had never slowed me down before, but now the question of why it *didn't* slow me down was bringing me to a complete halt. I couldn't keep my mind on a book or a writing assignment for longer than fifteen minutes.

As the weeks passed my concentration got worse, and for the first time I had to ask my dean to grant me late-paper extensions. The night before the final exam in second-year Chinese, which was by far my strongest subject, I panicked. I'm unprepared, I thought, and my teachers, who have been so good to me, will be disappointed. I'll get a bad grade and it will be the end of the world! I took a couple of No Doz pills and stayed up all night cramming, something I had never done before. Halfway through the exam my hands started shaking so badly that I couldn't form the characters. I sat in the chair staring at my hands without being able to control them, until the professor saw this and asked me outside.

"Are you all right?" he asked. I told him what was happening, and a pained look crossed his face. "How much of the exam did you complete?" he asked.

"Most of it, I think."

"Mark, everyone knows how much you've put into this class this year, and everyone knows you've had a bad shock recently. Go home and rest, for heaven's sake. There's really no need for you to be so worried about the exam."

I was grateful for this act of mercy, but by the time I got back to my room I began to feel stupid for having been so worried in the first place. What a grade-grubber I was! No wonder I was such a confused kid if my priorities were that out of whack. I mean, if you're going to face the great question of what your life means once you know it might end at any time with no regard for your aspirations, you ought to at least have the courage to get a B on a language exam.

That summer I decided not to go home. Charles McBirney, the professor who had rescued me from the exam, needed a part-time research assistant over the summer, and he introduced me to the owner of a Chinese restaurant in town who offered me a night job as a waiter. I rented an apartment in an unsavory but affordable neighborhood right next to the downtown YMCA, and only a few blocks away from the restaurant where I worked.

With school out for the summer I could wake up later and later. On a typical night I would come home from work at ten-thirty and fall right asleep. At one o'clock in the morning I would jerk awake from a nightmare and then toss and turn until three, when I would fall asleep and then start all over again. I usually crawled out of bed at noon. During the afternoons, if I wasn't working over at the Asian languages building, I usually drove out to one of the deserted beaches an hour or so east of New Haven and sat there until it was time to drive back and start work at the restaurant again.

What was the message? How do we go on? Wasn't this the very problem that had made my father the way he was? That was it; that was why I had to deal with this once and for all. This might be my last chance to do what I had set out to do so long ago: to bring order to the chaos, to make sense out of my life, to become happy the way my father hadn't. If I planned on keeping the sacred promise that we all make to ourselves at the threshold of adulthood—never to surrender to hypocrisy, complacency or mediocrity—I had to resolve this issue *now*. I owed it to my dad to go through with this to the bitter end and not give up this time. I felt I owed it to Michael, too. Poor kid, he wouldn't have the chance to do it himself.

I asked the big questions all day long, but instead of answers, there was only static in my head. It was almost like being stoned all the time, only it wasn't nearly as entertaining. Everything seemed drained of its color, flavor and interest. It was like waking up and finding myself in a black-and-white B movie, the kind you might see at two in the morning and watch without getting involved in the action or dialogue. You watch the flickering images because they attract your attention, but without much comprehension.

It was not a satisfying or pleasant sort of introspection, but I didn't resist it. On the contrary, I welcomed it; didn't all the historical figures I respected come to do what they did as a result of having answered these questions for themselves? Didn't my father once say he was glad that I asked questions like these, and didn't he say that I shouldn't expect the answers to come easily? Or something like that?

Although I never would have admitted it at the time, for some time I had cherished a whole body of romantic ideas about the nature of genius and inspiration, one of them being that you couldn't be a real artist if you hadn't had a nervous breakdown when you were young. The younger the better. However, my impression was that you couldn't just lower yourself into the depths whenever you felt like it; there had to be a plausible catalyst for the breakdown, a real or symbolic event that set off the psychological avalanche, and I could hardly ask for a more plausible one than the death of a childhood friend. I wasn't so monstrously selfish as to be glad that Michael had died, but I was selfish enough to convince myself that it was my duty, now that it had happened, to turn it into something positive.

By the time the fall semester began I was way too busy reading books about nihilism and Zen and staring out my window at the naked city to study Chinese at all. The semester was a disaster, to the point where I felt I had no choice but to drop out.

"Oh, no! Not this again!" my father said when I told him the news.

"At least he's got his high school diploma," my mother said, trying to cheer herself up.

"I'm not sure he does. Mark, you didn't actually graduate from there—did they ever send you a diploma?"

"No, I don't think so."

My mother's eyes froze in abject terror. "You never got your high school diploma? Oh, my God!" When my mother had nightmares, they usually came in one of three scenarios: having to walk across a field of dead birds; giving a concert without having prepared at all and with a strong wind blowing the music off her stand; and finding out that her kids never got their high school diplomas.

The next morning Mom called the high school, and the vice principal explained to her that I lacked one gym credit, so they could not issue a diploma for me. How I felt for that poor guy! I could see what was coming a mile away.

Mom hung up that phone so hard she practically tore it off the wall. When I was good, no one supported me with more enthusiasm than she did, but when I got myself into trouble, no one became half as angry or as determined to straighten things out. She went right to the car and drove herself to New Haven, where she had my dean write a letter attesting to the fact that I had lived for a year on the fifth floor of a dormitory building with no elevator, and simple arithmetic showed that the exercise I received from going to and from my room easily exceeded the state's requirements for a year of high school physical education. Mom brought this letter to the high school office, sat down in a chair and said she'd wait. She didn't get up again until the diploma was handed to her. When she came home and handed it to me her teeth were clenched so tight that two of her fillings rubbed together and sparked, and by God, I was on good behavior for the rest of that weekend.

The moral of my diploma story is that it's no coincidence that the toughest men in the world have the word "Mom" tattooed on their arms. Think about it.

Mom felt better when I got the diploma, but my year of darkness was just beginning. I continued my work with Professor McBirney a few hours a day and waited tables a few nights a week, but mostly I stayed in my room and brooded. I suppose I should have walked the streets late at night if I had really wanted to live on the edge, but with my experience in the cemetery still fresh in my memory, I thought it best to deconstruct myself in the safety of my apartment.

It got worse and worse. I slept fourteen, then sixteen hours a day, I found it almost impossible to get out of bed at all, and when I did I was always short of breath. I was frantically rereading all of my old Zen books, and even finding the Chinese versions of them in the library. To my disappointment and supreme aggravation, they were just as impenetrable in the original as they had been in the translation. *(The moon's reflection in the water is just a reflection. When you understand this, you understand this.)* I had majored in Chinese for nothing.

This. Thisness. *Be Here Now.* I forced myself to contemplate Thisness, I practiced Being Here Now, but all I could think of was *This* feels like *Shit* right *Now*. I saw flyers for a local Zen Buddhist temple and attended some of their morning meditation sessions, and sat through one of their harsh weekend retreats, but it wasn't for me. Why the robes? Why the incense and Buddha statues? Why the chanting in Korean? I'd done this already, and I didn't have the patience to try to take it seriously again; I felt I was running out of time.

No longer worrying about being prepared or not, I made an appointment to see Tungli Shen, the poet/scholar/philosopher I'd heard about for so many years. When I entered his office he was practicing calligraphy. He looked up and smiled, and just one look at his gentle face convinced me that he would have the answers I needed. I didn't want to burden him with my whole story, so for our meeting I brought along a single passage I'd chosen that I hoped got to the root of the whole problem of meaning and meaninglessness. It was written by Chuangtse, a Taoist who had lived in the third century B.C. I showed the quote to Mr. Shen and he translated it something like this:

Roosters call out, dogs bark
This is all we know.
Even the wisest men don't know where these voices come
*   from*
And can't explain why roosters call out and dogs bark
When they do. . . .

"What does it mean? I mean, what does it mean for *us*?" I asked him.

"Oh, I think it just means that there are lots of things we don't understand."

"Yes, but . . . how do we live with that? How do we live with not knowing?"

He smiled and closed his eyes. "Aha! Yes, that's the problem, isn't it? But that's just it; nobody knows how to do it! If you knew, then—well, then it wouldn't count as something that you don't understand, right?"

"Yes, but Mr. Shen, I don't understand the meaning of life, and I'm obviously unhappy. You say you don't understand the meaning of life, yet you're obviously happy. What am I missing?"

He laughed. "About fifty years of age, I think! A lot of these things seem to make better sense as you get older. Don't feel in such a hurry. That's what's making you so uncomfortable, I'll bet."

This wasn't what I wanted to hear. I decided to try with one more line of questioning. "So are you saying that this quote means something different to you now than when you were my age?"

"Yes. Sure."

"Can you tell me what it means to you now?"

He closed his eyes and laughed again. "You're smart! I hadn't thought of that. Still, it won't do you any good. That quote means something to me because . . . because of all the experiences I've had. Now when I read it, I put it together with my experiences. My childhood memories of Peking . . . such a beautiful place! Living in Hong Kong when the Japanese bombed it, seeing the atrocities of the war. Moving to this beautiful country—a foreign country to me!—raising my children here, teaching for many years. All of that is my answer to this quote. Your own life will be *your* answer to it. That's the way it works, I'm afraid. I don't know of any shortcut."

I was grateful for what Mr. Shen had told me, but instead of cheering me up, it struck me like a mortal blow. There was no point in my asking questions about mortality or meaning, he seemed to be saying, because in any case those questions would only be answered when I was really old. After this I was no longer in an existential dilemma; I was simply depressed. If I saw someone I knew approaching me on the street I pretended not to to see him and hurried off because small talk had become unbearable. Telephone conversations with my parents were agonizing. I could hear the concern in their voices, but instead of making me want to reassure them that I was fine, their worry made me feel guilty and defensive, so I sounded even worse than I really was. But I never thought of seeing a counselor or psychiatrist because to me this would have been both shameful and dangerous. Dangerous in the sense that I believed that any counselor would, for the sake of getting me back into school and into the system, do his best to seduce me into accepting the very sort of complacency and mediocrity that I had set out to destroy in myself. Also dangerous in the sense that a good counselor might see right through me and say, "You're not depressed because of your friend's death! You're like this because you're just disappointed that you can't be even more privileged than you already are by becoming some kind of sage! Frankly, we see a lot of this at the fancier schools, and it never ceases to disgust me." It did not occur to me that perhaps somewhere out there I could find a counselor who would be on my side, who would want to help me sort out my difficulties in a way I would have liked. It also never occurred to me to think that I might be wrong about complacency and mediocrity and what constituted the examined life. The more depressed I became, the more desperately I clung to the belief that I was right to be depressed. The possibility that I was seriously mistaken and going through all of this for nothing would have been unbearable.

I can only be grateful that Professor McBirney, whom I saw nearly every day at the Asian languages building, noticed I was in distress and took it upon himself to make sure I didn't go for long without friendly conversation. He treated me to several lunches a week, and as we became closer he began inviting me to dinner. He was not unlike my father in that he understood that one way to be a good friend to someone in need is to be a good listener, and he let me bore him for literally hundreds of hours. It helped me to be able to express my thoughts to someone, and the fact that a full professor took such a keen interest in my philosophical gropings was the one source of self-esteem I had left. But many years later he confessed, to my great relief, that ever since graduate school he had possessed the ability to appear to be listening when in fact he was working out grammar or translation problems, so I hadn't tortured him as much as I'd thought.

The months crawled by, the weather got colder and wetter, the days grew shorter, and I slept more and more. By December I was at the end of my endurance. I had been so uncomfortable for so long that I became desperate for some kind of relief. But what relief was there for this sort of thing?

Naturally, in earlier moments of intense unhappiness (as when Dad found my pot plants), I had imagined myself jumping off a cliff or slitting my throat, but that was always more of a revenge or punishment fantasy than anything else, and it passed in a matter of hours or even minutes, like a mild fever. But now the idea of oblivion—permanent and total relief—came to have a kind of sensible appeal. Instead of being an impulsive fantasy of desperation, it began to seem like the only merciful response to a problem that had already turned me into a zombie and was only going to get worse. I didn't want to drag anyone else down with me, and I knew I couldn't stand what I had gotten myself into for much longer.

It seemed like the rational choice, but as long as my parents were alive it was a hopelessly impractical one. The thought of what it would do to them was so revolting, so inexpressibly obscene, that I could only shake my head and think, Maybe tomorrow I'll come up with something, maybe tomorrow a miracle will happen.

On an impulse, one Saturday afternoon I asked Professor McBirney if I could borrow his car for the weekend and visit my parents. If I was keeping myself suspended in a living hell for their sakes, I figured, they could at least entertain and feed me every once in a while. He agreed. I thanked him, drove home and spent that evening on the couch wrapped up in the green blanket, watching Dad work on a watercolor. As usual, that night I had a stupid anxiety dream—only, this one was so stupid that I made myself remember it when I woke up so I could tell it to my dad in the morning, thinking he'd get a kick out of it.

In the dream I had been invited by NASA to give a lecture to a blue-ribbon committee of engineers gathered to discuss the construction of a space capsule that would carry a man to the planet Jupiter and back. Because of my extensive experience as an astronaut on several of the Mars missions, the engineers wanted to know what suggestions I had for the Jupiter capsule. After I'd been introduced, I opened up my briefcase and produced a sheaf of diagrams I'd prepared showing exactly how to build the new capsule. As I lowered the first one into the projector, nervous laughter filled the room. I looked at the screen on the wall and saw, to my initial confusion, a crude drawing of a cardboard box.

It must be a prank, I thought, examining my pile of diagrams. When I held them in my hand they looked exactly as I'd drawn them, elaborate and precise, but as soon as I fitted each sheet into the projector, they turned into sketches of the cardboard box I'd sat in as a child dreaming that I was an astronaut. The nervous laughter in the audience turned to annoyed silence, then to an ominous murmur. At last the director of NASA asked me to step down. I tried to protest, but two men in dark suits with reflective sunglasses and tiny ear radios picked me up roughly and threw me out of the auditorium.

"What do you think of that?" I asked Dad.

"Pretty stupid, all right," he said distractedly, getting his brushes ready for the afternoon's work.

Obviously he hadn't been paying full attention; otherwise he would have given more of a response. I didn't say anything for a few minutes, while he picked up where he'd left off on the painting the day before. It was of the woods outside our living-room window at night, done almost entirely in shades of black except for two bright green plastic lawn chairs, facing each other and glowing eerily in the light coming from our house.

"You know what I want to call it?" Dad asked, looking at the painting and grinning.

"What?"

" 'They Think We're Only Lawn Chairs.' " He chuckled, but I, feeling angry that he hadn't shown more interest in my dream, didn't respond. When he started touching up one of the chairs, I decided to return to the subject.

"You know what's weird about that dream, though?"

"What?"

"It's kind of true. I mean, I am a phony, if you think about it."

"How are you a phony, Mark?"

"Think about it, Dad! I'm always trying to change myself into somebody I'm not. It's the story of my life."

He nodded and kept painting. I suppose he thought I hadn't finished speaking. I was annoyed with him, but something about his way of handling the conversation—he hadn't exactly rushed to disagree with me about my being a phony—provoked me to continue.

"Look at what I've done since I was thirteen: first I tried to become a kung fu master, then a concert cellist, now a professor of Chinese, and none of these are really me. I might as well put on a cape and pretend to be Superman; it wouldn't be much more ridiculous. Other people do things gradually, but not me. I don't want to have to take little steps to get somewhere; it's always the Big Leap for me, always the Complete Transformation. Of course I don't ever get there because I'm a quitter."

To drive the point home, I went on to produce the evidence that I was a quitter, evidence that also showed that I consistently quit things whenever I was about to be revealed as a phony:

1) I had quit martial arts because kung fu hadn't turned

me into a fearless warrior, something that any idiot could have told me I would never be.

2) After ten years of cello training, most of which I spent trying to please him and Mom, I heard Yo Yo Ma play once, which made me quit. If I couldn't be him, I apparently didn't want to bother at all, though any fool could have told me that Yo Yo Ma, besides being a genius, had been practicing six hours a day since he was three years old. But did I think I should have to work that hard? No way!

3) After becoming a Chinese major because it was the one subject I had a head start in and could therefore look smarter than I really was by focusing on it, I became convinced that reading Chinese philosophical texts in the original language would transform me into Tungli Shen. When I finally did read some of those texts in the original, however, and remained unenlightened, I lost all interest in Chinese culture.

4) (Most ludicrous of all) I had quit college because I was too depressed over being a quitter to concentrate on my homework.

Lastly I reminded my father of the pointlessness of everything, just in case he'd forgotten. "We're just big clumps of atoms jiggling around in patterns. It's just like you always used to say: We think we're so special, but then if we give it any careful thought we realize, *Who do we think we're kidding?*"

Dad didn't look as if he was going to contradict me on this point, so I continued. "It's finally dawned on me that all the people I like or respect have admitted to not knowing any of the answers to the great questions of life and death. Still, they all seem to live with that; they move forward. But I can't! I'm constantly feeling, Is this all there

is? Even when I was little I was like that, which is probably why I was always daydreaming. Now I can't daydream anymore because I'm old enough to know that all
of that is just kidding myself, it's just a smoke screen I
throw up to distract myself. Now that I don't even have
that anymore, all I can see is fifty or sixty years of drudgery, after which I'll probably drop dead in a retirement
home. That what it's all about, isn't it?"

I paused dramatically, waiting for either a verbal response or at least applause. It had been a devastatingly
good speech, I thought. But Dad didn't even look up from
his watercolor, so I decided to force him to speak.

"Jesus, Dad, you're a social worker," I said, allowing
myself to feel angry. "You must have something to say
about all this."

At last my father put down his brush and raised his
head to look at me. He pushed his reading glasses a bit
higher up his nose, and examined me for what seemed like
a long time. He raised one eyebrow, then lowered it; his
mouth opened slightly, then closed again. He seemed to
be running through several possible responses before set-
tling on one.

At last his face broke into a grin. "Welcome," he said,
shrugging.

He waited to see what I would do. When I found that I
really had no choice but to grin back, he nodded, then
resumed painting.

EPILOGUE

A person is never himself but always a mask; a
person never owns his own person, but always
represents another, by whom he is possessed. And
the other that one is, is always ancestors.
                                        —NORMAN O. BROWN

In June of 1993 a trio of astronomers discovered a
comet that had broken into several pieces on its last trip
around the sun. Soon after they announced their discovery, other scientists observing the comet realized, by calculating its speed, position and trajectory, that the pieces
would crash into the planet Jupiter in July 1994. The collisions, they said, would be of such magnitude that if they
were to occur here on earth, civilization as we know it
would cease to exist. Some scientists predicted the impacts would be so violent that we would be able to see
evidence of the destruction through even amateur telescopes, four hundred million miles away from the action.
Other scientists insisted that the comet fragments were
too small, and would be swallowed up by Jupiter's cloudy
atmosphere and liquid-hydrogen surface like marbles
dropped into a colossal milk shake. They warned astronomers not to get their hopes up for a cosmic display.

"We'll never see it from here," my dad said, agreeing as always with the naysayers, but that didn't stop him from driving five hundred miles from Tucson, Arizona, where he and my mother moved after he retired, to California with his new telescope so that he and I could watch from the top of Mount Wilson just in case. I already had the old telescope with me in Los Angeles, which he'd given me, along with a good pair of binoculars, as a wedding present. We would set up the two telescopes side by side and compare the optics.

Dad's dream of retirement had finally come true, thirty-five years after he'd entered the workforce, and long after the last of our Volkswagen buses had rusted out and been towed away. For this comet-viewing trip he drove a Plymouth Voyager that tended, in spite of sharing its name with the highest-flying NASA probe of all, to stall at high altitudes. He'd brought this problem to the dealer's attention many times without any positive results. The day before the comet was to hit we tried taking it up Mount Wilson on a dry run to find a good place to set up our telescopes, and sure enough the Voyager quit voyaging before we reached the top.

"Buy American," he grumbled as we coasted back down to L.A. "I'd like to shove this car up Lee Iacocca's ass." The next night we played it safe and took my Toyota Corolla. This meant we could only take his more compact telescope.

Fifteen years had passed since Dad had delivered his memorable "Welcome" speech in Connecticut. As rites of passage go, it could hardly compare in terms of sophistication or drama to such time-tested ceremonies as First Communion, the bar mitzvah or adult circumcision without painkillers. Still, it worked; that moment had proved to be the watershed experience of my adolescence. As a child I could always count on my father to understand me, to know what it was like, to put himself in my shoes. On that afternoon a cycle was completed: he had let me know that I had finally managed to get *his* shoes on. Like the Wizard of Oz pinning a medal to the Cowardly Lion's chest, my father merely drew attention, in his streamlined way, to what I already knew.

Another circular aspect to our exchange on that day was that after I'd tried, in a psychological sense, to get away from him for so many years, it was both ironic and cheering to run into Dad at the farthest point of my journey. If Norman O. Brown is right and we really aren't ourselves, if we really are just masks representing our ancestors, my experience shows that there is a positive side to discovering that your individual soul is actually more of a corporation: being possessed means never having to say you're alone.

At the same time, standing in my father's shoes made it clear to me that while we had a lot in common, I was not entirely like him after all. The shoes didn't quite fit. In fact, most people who know our family insist that in terms of personality, I resemble my father's oldest brother, Ray, the wildly extroverted interior decorator, more than my wildly introverted father. But that's another story.

I am a synthetic pessimist, not the real thing. I was seriously depressed over the pointlessness of existence for a year, but after I'd reached the point of exhaustion and knew there was no use going any further with it, I got sick of thinking about pointlessness. I didn't solve the problem; I simply lost interest. I'd had enough of staring out the window of my apartment. I went back to college the following year and tried to switch my major to English, only to learn that I didn't have enough credits to do so; I had to finish up in Chinese. I took the attitude that I would do so for the diploma and not take it too seriously, and as a result ended up enjoying myself more than I would have predicted.

For a senior project I translated a group of Tungli Shen's vernacular Chinese poems, which gave me the opportunity to meet with him once a week for a whole year and chat over pizza and coffee in a restaurant across the street from the Asian languages building. It was a low-stress project; I liked the poems, and I could relax knowing that if I had any questions about any of them, I had access to the world's undisputed authority on the subject.

Once he retired, my father was able to devote all his energies to his three major interests: painting, astronomy and getting angry whenever he reads in the paper or sees on television that public interest in the supernatural is on the rise.

"Did you hear that, Martha? Colleges are offering courses in *astrology*." This was the afternoon of the comet crash, and he was anxious about our trip up Mount Wilson. Would it become cloudy? Would we get a flat tire? What if a carjacker figured out that there might be a few astronomers on the dark, lonely road up to the famous observatory?

Dad switched the channel, only to get coverage of a Christian youth rally to welcome the pope. The vein on his forehead looked ready to blow. *"This* guy! *This* is the guy who *only now* admits that Galileo was right, four hundred years after everybody else gets it straight. Yet he insists that there is *no question* that God thinks birth control is a bad idea. What is the *matter* with people?"

"Oh, Dad," I said, knowing it wasn't really a question but falling for the bait anyway. "Lots of people find it comforting to think there's a Plan, and a Planner who cares. Why should people like us spoil it for them?"

"Well, sure it's comforting, but that doesn't mean they should believe it! I mean, if some people want to believe the Bible, or tarot cards, or those pathetic hustlers in the infomercials for Dial-a-Psychic, fine, but at least let 'em keep it in the privacy of their homes. Why does it have to make the news? If I wanted fairy tales, I'd get the Fairy Tale Channel. This is CNN, dammit. Why don't they have anything on about Jupiter? The event of the century is about to happen and I have to watch a man who thinks he's qualified to speak for God ride around in a motorized, bulletproof soap bubble with a dumb hat on. Bullshit!"

I tend to agree with Dad on these matters, but my sense of shame forces me to tone it down; it would be a little cheeky for a guy who used to wear a baldhead wig to make fun of the pope's hat.

The hours crept by. We started driving right after dinner and got to the top of Mount Wilson just as Jupiter and Venus became visible in the evening sky. There were no clouds, fortunately. We set up Dad's telescope and had a look. There was nothing on the surface of Jupiter that either of us could see.

"I knew it," Dad said, nodding.

"It's still early."

We looked for several of our old summer favorites like the Lagoon and Ring nebulas, but the moonlight drowned them out. We had to be satisfied wandering through the thick parts of the Milky Way, marveling at the incomprehensible number of stars in our local arm of our spiral galaxy. If we could somehow view the whole galaxy at once, we would see more than four hundred billion of them. And the distances! If we could build a rocket that traveled a million miles an hour, it would still take us three thousand years to reach Alpha Centauri, the star closest to us. And the other stars? If a group of people could travel at the speed of light—a million miles every five seconds—they would have to celebrate thirty thousand birthdays together before reaching the center of our own galaxy. What about the other galaxies? There are at least a hundred billion of them out there; imagine how long it would take to put together even a modest tour.

Those of us attracted to astronomy look at the stars because we can't help it; when we look at the night sky we are reminded that we are staring into the unknown, and that bothers us, leaves us feeling anxious and incomplete. We feel compelled to try, by gazing through our telescopes, to make the unknown known, to bring it into the realm of the familiar. We know that the astronauts and cosmonauts who have actually seen with their own eyes the earth from space all agree on one thing: concepts such as the brotherhood of humanity, the interdependence of all life and the fragility of our planet suddenly became much more real for them than they had been before. For them, this island earth went from being an intellectual experience to a personal one.

Astronomers would like to make the universe a personal experience, even though they know it cannot be done. To hope that any of us could experience the emptiness beyond the farthest galaxies, not to mention what might lie in universes entirely separate from our own—or, for that matter, the worlds hidden within each subatomic particle—is unrealistic given the very real limitations of time and space and our own senses.

Yet we keep looking through our telescopes and microscopes. Why, if we know we cannot be satisfied? Perhaps this question is related to the one I put to my father: How do we live if we know we must die? Why bother with any of this, since none of it will matter when the sun burns up and the earth turns into a cold cinder? Why bother with anything?

The provisional answer to this question is: Because bothering is still the best game in town. I would even argue that for human beings, bothering is the *only* game in town. Stephen Hawking, the physicist, was asked if he thought everything in the universe, including our thoughts, behavior and sense of free will, was determined by the fundamental laws of physics. Yes, he answered; the universe is determined, but the equations are so staggeringly complex that no one can ever hope to solve them. He wrote:

> I have noticed that even people who claim that everything is predestined and that we can do nothing to change it look before they cross the road. . . . One cannot base one's conduct on the idea that everything is determined because one does not know what has been determined. Instead, one has to adopt the effective theory that one has free will and that one is responsible for one's actions. This theory is not very good at predicting human behavior, but we adopt it because there is no chance of solving the equations arising from the fundamental laws. There is also a Darwinian reason that we believe in free will: a society in

which the individual feels responsible for his or her actions is more likely to work together and survive to spread its values.

If this is true, then the theory of natural selection would explain why so many of us do care, why so many of us find that the struggle to understand ourselves and the world is worthwhile: because over many generations, we have been bred to be insatiably curious. Those of our ancestors who gave a damn and learned to understand the world a little better survived to reproduce more often than the ones who didn't. So here we are: people who are genetically designed to wonder how things work, born into a world far too complex and far too chaotic to ever be completely understood.

Half an hour passed before Dad and I pointed the telescope at Jupiter again. This time we both thought we saw something coming into view on one of the edges, but we couldn't be sure. The minutes crawled by. As Jupiter turned on its axis, the far edge of the planet slowly came more clearly into view, and sure enough, there was a round, dark spot on the surface that hadn't been there before. We were exhilarated.

"Wait a minute," Dad said, coming back from the car where he had checked a packet of the information he'd sent away for from *Sky and Telescope* magazine. He looked back through the telescope. "Shit," he said. "This isn't it."

The spot we were looking at was on the wrong hemisphere! We'd heard on the radio before we left the house that several of the comet fragments had hit, and had landed on the northern hemisphere as predicted. Together we checked the packet of information; no doubt about it, the comet would strike the northern hemisphere. We looked back through the telescope. Now there were two of the dark spots, but they were on the *southern* hemisphere.

"Are you sure that couldn't be the northern hemisphere?" I asked. The uncertainty came from the fact that reflecting telescopes show their images in reverse; when I looked at the spots they were on the top of the planet, so it *felt* as if they were on the northern hemisphere, even though I knew better.

"Nope. I know what these are," Dad said, sighing.

"What?"

"They're shadows. Two of Jupiter's moons must be in front of the planet. Look how round and distinct those spots are, and how huge. There's no way that the comet could have done that. They're just shadows."

We were both disappointed, but the night was still young. We searched the northern hemisphere for hours, even making sketches every fifteen minutes in case something came up that we didn't notice immediately, but there was nothing. Both of us kept looking back at those two dark spots; what if we were wrong somehow, and they were the real thing after all? We wanted to believe this, but *wanting* something to be true isn't the same thing as *believing* it is true. At midnight, feeling tired and realizing we had a long drive home, we gave up.

We all crave certainty, we dream of serenity, and we all want to discover our true identities. The Zen people like to ask, What was your Original Face before you were born? Who were you before your parents taught you how to be "yourself"? Most of us tend to feel that if it could be proved, once and for all, that we shall never know the answers to those questions, and that our species was simply not designed for serenity or certainty, then our whole human enterprise—the search for meaning and understanding—would be rendered futile and pathetic. But is this really true? Doesn't it make sense that if we were designed to search, there could be nothing more horrifying for our species than to reach an end to all these searches? Wouldn't this make all of us incredibly bored, not to mention boring? Can anyone imagine anything duller than not having anything to wonder about? The possibility of our being forever unable to know everything all at once may be the best design feature of this whole human experiment.

When Dad and I got home from Mount Wilson, Mom and Jessica were still up.

"Did you have fun?" Mom asked.

"We didn't see much, I'm afraid."

"Too bad! Jessica and I watched *Tales from the Crypt.* It was so *awful,* but I kind of liked it. Do we get that channel in Tucson, Joe?"

I had left my mother, the Bach specialist, alone with my wife, who thinks that Jason from the *Friday the 13th* movies is a postmodern antihero, for a mere six hours, and look what had happened! I imagined having to do an intervention, storming her practice room and finding her watching *Hellraiser* videos instead of playing the harpsichord.

. . .

The next morning I got up and found my dad sitting in the living room reading the paper. "You're not going to believe this," he said, shaking his head.

"What?"

He pointed to a photograph of Jupiter taken from the Hubble Space Telescope. "We were looking at it last night. Those spots. That was it."

"But . . . ?"

"It's the new telescope. It's a Cassegrain, not like our old Newtonian. I forgot it has a prism right in front of the eyepiece to correct for the reversed image. I'm still not used to it, I guess."

We had been looking at the spectacle of the century all night, but without being able to enjoy it.

"That's not all," Dad continued. "The weather forecast for tonight is clouds."

"Oh. Bummer."

"You could say that."

We stared at the pictures splashed all over the front page. There the spots were, just as we'd seen them, each of them bigger than the earth.

"Astronomers all over the world were elated and amazed," the article raved. "Few expected it to be this spectacular."

"This is like the eclipse in Canada all over again," Dad said.

"No, it's not that bad. We *did* see it, after all. We just didn't, you know—"

"Really see it," he interrupted.

Which was when I saw the opportunity sitting there like a plump, flightless bird. It was hardly sporting, but I couldn't resist. "Don't be crushed, Dad. You see, not everything works out the way you want it to. You learn to live with it, though."

He looked up from the paper and gave me a long, slow burn with his eyes.

"Smart-ass."

MARK SALZMAN'S previous books include *Iron &
Silk,* an account of the two years he spent in China
teaching English and studying martial arts, and
two novels: *The Laughing Sutra* and *The Soloist,*
which was a finalist for the Los Angeles Times
Book Prize for Fiction. Mr. Salzman lives with his
wife and their various animals in Los Angeles. Besides writing, he practices the cello every day in
the hope of one day being able to play well enough
so that his cats don't flee the room. Though he
enjoyed revisiting his past in this book, Mr. Salzman is grateful that so few photographs of him as
a teenager survive.

This book was set in Sabon, a typeface designed by the well-known German typographer Jan Tschichold (1902–74). Sabon's design is based upon the original letter forms of Claude Garamond and was created specifically to be used for three sources: foundry type for hand composition, Linotype, and Monotype. Tschichold named his typeface for the famous Frankfurt typefounder Jacques Sabon, who died in 1580.